T0354337

THE
DANGER
OF
SELF-RIGHTEOUSNESS

EMMANUEL ATOE

WESTBOW
PRESS®
A DIVISION OF THOMAS NELSON
& ZONDERVAN

Copyright © 2024 Emmanuel Atoe.

All rights reserved. No part of this book may be used or reproduced by any means, graphic, electronic, or mechanical, including photocopying, recording, taping or by any information storage retrieval system without the written permission of the author except in the case of brief quotations embodied in critical articles and reviews.

This book is a work of non-fiction. Unless otherwise noted, the author and the publisher make no explicit guarantees as to the accuracy of the information contained in this book and in some cases, names of people and places have been altered to protect their privacy.

WestBow Press books may be ordered through booksellers or by contacting:

WestBow Press
A Division of Thomas Nelson & Zondervan
1663 Liberty Drive
Bloomington, IN 47403
www.westbowpress.com
844-714-3454

Because of the dynamic nature of the Internet, any web addresses or links contained in this book may have changed since publication and may no longer be valid. The views expressed in this work are solely those of the author and do not necessarily reflect the views of the publisher, and the publisher hereby disclaims any responsibility for them.

Any people depicted in stock imagery provided by Getty Images are models, and such images are being used for illustrative purposes only.
Certain stock imagery © Getty Images.

All Scripture quotations are taken from the King James
Version of the Bible and used with permission.

ISBN: 979-8-3850-1589-4 (sc)
ISBN: 979-8-3850-1590-0 (e)

Library of Congress Control Number: 2023924680

Print information available on the last page.

WestBow Press rev. date: 03/18/2024

SPONSORSHIP PAGE

THIS BOOK IS SPONSORED BY

....

....

AS A GIFT TO

....

....

ON THIS DAY

....

'Each one must give as he has decided in his heart,
not reluctantly or under compulsion,
for God loves a cheerful giver.'
(2 Corinthians 9:7, ESV)

DEDICATION

This book is dedicated to the Righteous in Christ

A special thanks go to Prophet Angelo Grasso for his encouragement
to minister the Word of God in Italian Language.

The LORD bless you and keep you; The LORD make His face
shine upon you and be gracious to you; The LORD lift His
countenance upon you and give you peace, in Jesus' Name. Amen.

Always be full of joy in the Lord. I say it again - rejoice!

CONTENTS

INTRODUCTION

The enemy and his cohorts specialize in deceiving people and preventing them from coming to the knowledge of the Truth – the Word of God. The truth of the gospel sets free, illuminates, and guides. Ignorance, misinformation, lies, and deceit are tools in the hands of the devil. He uses these tools to kill, steal, and destroy. One of the areas that the enemy has succeeded in deceiving and leading any people to hell is in making them believe that, without God, they can be righteous by their own efforts or charitable deeds. This is called self-righteousness, and it is one of man's greatest sins and failings today.

In his encounter with Eve in the Garden of Eden, the serpent twisted the commandment God gave her and Adam, confused, and beguiled her until she swallowed the lethal bait of disobedience, hook, line, and sinker. The consequences of that enemy's attack on our first parents are still with us today. Though satan tried it with Jesus Christ in His earthly sojourn and ministry (Matthew 4), he failed woefully because the Lord responded to his attack with a superior weapon – the word of God.

In the same vein, today, the enemy is attacking and twisting the truths of God's word on righteousness, making many people fall into the error of self-righteousness with its attendant grave consequences. Unlike many people, the enemy knows that God hates self-righteousness, condemns it, and judges or punishes it. It is disheartening that many people, including believers, are self-righteous but they do not know. The truth is that their ignorance will not exempt them from the divine consequences of self-righteousness. It is the responsibility of all believers and unbelievers to seek, know, apply the truth, and let the truth set them free. Beloved, you need to acquire divine knowledge about righteousness as well as self-righteousness and avoid the dangers of self-righteousness or pray it out of your life.

Today, God's word on righteousness is clear. The gospel truth that believers need to buy and not sell is that no person can be righteous by his or her own effort or good deeds. Righteousness is given to us by God. The reason is that all have sinned and fallen short of the glory of God (Romans3:23). Man, through his sin and his fall, lost his right standing with God. The grace of God and faith in God are two criteria that now qualify him for the gift of righteousness. It is a gift! God demands that we should be righteous. He detests and punishes unrighteousness in all its ramifications. However, it does not end there. Just as unrighteousness is sin, self-righteousness is also a fatal sin and God judges it.

Today, many believers are well-acquainted with the meaning, importance, manifestations, and rewards of righteousness. They also know what unrighteousness stands for and its numerous consequences. However, little is known about self-righteousness, its causes, manifestations as well as dangers or consequences.

This eye-opening book turns the spotlight on self-righteousness, stressing that it is capable of preventing millions of souls that should be won for Christ from being lost or making even believers who are its victims miss heaven.

The Bible affirms that God sent His word, healed them, and delivered them from their destruction (Psalm 107:20). It also affirms that by knowledge shall the righteous be delivered. (Proverbs 11:9 NASB1995). Righteousness is a gift from God to us, to make us become everything good and glorious that God purposed for His children before the foundation of the earth was laid. Conversely, pride and self-righteousness are of satan, the opposition. The self-righteous attitude is a rebellion against God and is condemnable. It attracts disastrous consequences from God.

Many people, unknowingly, are guilty of self-righteousness. Many do not know that they are wallowing in it. There is connection between self-righteousness and pride. The truth is that the same God who detests pride and resists the proud but gives grace to the humble also condemns self-righteousness and handsomely rewards righteousness. In His life and ministry, Jesus also condemned the self-righteousness of the Pharisees and Sadducees on several occasions (Matthew 23).

Today, many believers are caught in the web and trap of self-righteousness and need to be rescued from them. To achieve this, they need divine knowledge. The word of God is the key to our deliverance and healing! In this book, the illuminating power of God's word is used to expose self-righteousness and its manifestations. Similarly, the all-conquering power of God's word is used to stop its dangers and destroy its consequences in people's lives. If righteousness would exalt a nation (Proverbs 14:34) and its rewards would greatly bless the lives of God's children, self-righteousness and all its consequences must be checkmated and rooted out of the lives of people, their homes, the Church, and nations.

The salient messages of this book are clear: Self-righteousness angers God and has disastrous consequences. You do not have to be caught in the dragnet and web of self-righteousness. Self-righteousness and pride do not have to send you to hellfire. You can be free from the spirit, attitude, and consequences of self-righteousness. I encourage you to read this life-changing book and mine its unquantifiable treasures!

ONE

UNDERSTANDING
SELF-RIGHTEOUSNESS

C hristians are called to live righteous lives. Proverbs 21:21 affirms that whoever pursues righteousness and love finds life, prosperity, and honor. They are also enjoined to bear the fruits of righteousness and encourage others to be righteous. Similarly, Matthew 6:23 says, "Seek ye first the Kingdom of God and HIS righteousness…" God does not want us to be self-righteous. Isaiah 64:6 speaks of the righteousness of the people as filthy rags in the sight of God. There is no righteousness except the righteousness of God. As Christians, we are to shun and condemn unrighteousness as well as self-righteousness. God's wrath is revealed against all ungodliness and unrighteousness of men. This is because we have no righteousness of our own. We can only be made righteous by God.

As believers, we must know the meaning and importance of true righteousness. The following cardinal points will shed more light on this issue:

1. True righteousness means trusting God: One major hallmark of those who are righteous is that they demonstrate unwavering trust in God. They do not exhibit false or self-confidence. They depend on God and trust Him with all their hearts. They do not lean on their understanding. Rather, they acknowledge God in all their ways and surrender all to Him. Abraham is a good example of a righteous believer. In Galatians 3:6, the Bible affirms that he believed God, and it was accounted to him as righteousness.

Conversely, the self-righteous believes that he has no need for God and does not trust or depend on Him.

2. True righteousness means not having one's own righteousness... but ... of God: Apostle Paul affirmed this in Philippians 3:9 when he said, "... be found in him, not having my own righteousness, which *is* from the law, but that which *is* through faith in Christ, the righteousness which is from God by faith."

3. Trues righteousness is in believing and affirming the words of God in Titus 3:5: It is important to know and always remember that no excellent work we do on our part can qualify us or make us righteous before God. It is only by His mercy and grace that He imputed His righteousness to us and saved us. We did nothing to earn it; it is His gift to us. "But Not by works of righteousness which we have done, but according to his mercy he saved us."

Christians should believe in God's righteousness and reject our own righteousness. A person who believes in God's righteousness rejects his own righteousness. Apostle Paul is a shining example in this regard. The Bible affirms this in Philippians 3:7-10 when Paul said, "But what things were gain to me, those I counted loss for Christ. Yea doubtless, and I count all things but loss for the excellency of the knowledge of Christ Jesus my Lord: for whom I have suffered the loss of all things, and do count them but dung, that I may win Christ. And be found in him, not having mine own righteousness, which is of the law, but that which is through the faith of Christ, the righteousness which is of God by faith: That I may know him, and the power of his resurrection, and the fellowship of his sufferings, being made conformable unto his death."

As Christians, who believe God is righteous, we should rejoice in the righteousness that comes from God. Also, a person who believes in God's righteousness rejoices in the righteousness that comes from God. In Romans 5:1, the Bible underscores this point, "Therefore being justified by faith, we have peace with God through our Lord Jesus Christ." Here Apostle Paul reaffirms our justification as believers is as a result of the faith we exercise in the finished, atoning, and substitutionary work of Jesus and not our own work of righteousness. The Bible corroborates this in Titus 3:5-7, "Not by works of righteousness which we have done, but according to his mercy he saved us, by the washing of regeneration, and renewing of the Holy Ghost, which he shed on us abundantly through Jesus Christ our Saviour. That being justified by his grace, we should be made heirs according to the hope of eternal life."

WHAT DOES IT MEAN TO BE SELF-RIGHTEOUS?

The word "righteous" is used throughout the Bible to describe those who conform their heart and lives to godly living. However, the term "self-righteous" does not belong solely to those who follow God. Anyone can be self-righteous if they believe their ways are the right ways, and everyone else's ways are wrong. Self-righteousness attitudes are rampant as people become intent on proving their moral superiority.

Self-righteousness is thinking that we are better than anyone else because we think that we have done a lot of good things. We fool ourselves that God needs us because we are good, when in reality it is us who need God. Our righteousness is nothing compared to the righteousness of God. Isaiah 54:6 says that our righteousness is like filthy rags. No amount of good things that we do can ever erase the penalty of sin we have committed.

The cause of self-righteousness is simply because we think we are better than others and God – that our righteousness earned us our salvation. We need to realise that it is God's righteousness that has given us life and grace to be part of His kingdom.

In the light of the Gospel, self-righteousness has the following meanings and interpretations:

1. It is to be convinced that of your own righteousness especially in contrast with the actions and beliefs of others. It is to be narrow-mindedly moralistic.

3

2. It is to act superior to your peers because you believe your moral standards are perfect. This 'moral smugness' is often condescending by nature and is usually found offensive by others."

3. It is to believe you are better and more moral than other people. Often, this is expressed annoyingly or offensively.

4. It is the sin of justifying yourself. The "self" tacked on to "righteousness" is the problem. When you start justifying self, you get into trouble. For example, those who are self-righteous are quick to point out the sins in others to justify their own shortcomings, insecurities, and sinful behaviour.

5. It is to believe that you are better than and morally superior to someone else. This description of a self-righteous person sounds like a lot of "Christians." If you call yourself a "Christian," you really need to examine your heart on the subject. Christian self-righteousness is the worst kind and so repulsive. The exact opposite of what Christ really meant for us to be. A true Christian never boasts of his own righteousness because a true Christian knows he doesn't have any through his own initiative. A true Christian knows from where his righteousness really comes.

6. It is tantamount to hypocrisy. The Message describes self-righteous hypocrisy this way in Romans 2:1-2: "Those people are on a dark spiral downward. But if you think that leaves you on the high ground where you can point your finger at others, think again. Every time you criticize someone, you condemn yourself. It takes one to know one. Judgmental criticism of others is a well-known way of escaping detection in your own crimes and misdemeanours. But God isn't so easily diverted. He sees right through all such smoke screens and holds you to what you've done.

7. It is driven and engendered by pride. Those who are self-righteous are often full of pride. Self-righteousness focuses on the outward behaviors of others rather than one's own heart. These want attention for their imagined "righteousness," such as the Pharisees in the Bible. Jesus says, "Be careful not to practice your righteousness in front of others to be seen by them (Matthew 6:1 NIV)." The Pharisees' self-righteousness

and pride prevented them from recognizing and seeing their need of the Savior.

8. It is fed by judging others. In pastoral work, the people who often tout "judge not" are often the people who judge the most. Not only do they judge others, but they make up their own rules for judging others. They think they are better than others based on actions. They blame others for their own sins, and they justify themselves by judging others. In Matthew 7:3-5, the Bible says, "Why do you look at the speck of sawdust in your brother's eye and pay no attention to the plank in your own eye? How can you say to your brother, 'Let me take the speck out of your eye,' when all the time there is a plank in your own eye? You hypocrite, first take the plank out of your own eye, and then you will see clearly to remove the speck from your brother's eye."

9. It makes you believe that you are righteous. They arrogantly put themselves in the position of God bestowing judgment on whomever they see fit. Whether you are or are not a Christian, you can easily fall into the trap of self-righteousness and the sin of justifying yourself. As you read this, if you're thinking of other people, stop. Consider yourself. Think through your own actions. Apply this to you. The self-righteous will have a difficult time examining their heart. That might be a clue that it is you.

10. It repels people. A self-righteous person will make you feel guilty, unrighteous, uncomfortable, and condemned. As a result it draws people away from the self-righteous. On the other hand, genuine righteousness draws people toward you. Jesus Christ is the perfect example of a righteous Being. He draws people toward Him and not repel off.

11. It is not knowing about God's righteousness. It is seeking to establish one's righteousness and failing to subject oneself to the righteousness of God (Romans 10:3).

12. It is to love and cling to self-justification. This was the pitiable state of the man who encountered Jesus in Luke 10:29 and asked Him, "Who is my neighbour?"

13. It is to have confidence in the flesh and in the righteousness which is in the law (Philippians 3:4-6).

   "Though I also might have confidence in the flesh. If anyone else thinks he may have confidence in the flesh, I more so: circumcised the eighth day, of the stock of Israel, *of* the tribe of Benjamin, a Hebrew of the Hebrews; concerning the law, a Pharisee; concerning zeal, persecuting the church; concerning the righteousness which is in the law, blameless."

14. It is to say you have no sin, deceiving yourself and lacking truth. 1 John 1:8 says, "If we say that we have no sin, we deceive ourselves, and the truth is not in us." Self-righteousness and pride are Siamese twins. The self-righteous say that they have cleansed their hearts and are pure from sin.

15. The self-righteous, like Ephraim, says that they have become rich and found wealth for themselves. They believe that they are self-made and everything they achieve comes solely from and by their efforts. They believe that they have no iniquity or sin.

   Hosea 12:8

   "And Ephraim said, 'Surely, I have become rich, I have found wealth for myself; In all my labours. They shall find in me no iniquity that is sin."

16. It is to believe that all your ways are clean in your eyes. The self-righteous leave out God's judgment or assessment of them and their motives (Prov. 16:2). This is also tied to Jeremiah 2:34-35).

   Prov. 16:2

   "All the ways of a man *are* pure in his own eyes, But the LORD weighs the spirits."

   Jeremiah 2:34-35

   "Also on your skirts is found the blood of the lives of the poor innocents. I have not found it by secret search, but plainly on all these things. Yet you say, 'Because I am innocent, surely His anger shall turn from me. Behold, I will plead My case against you because you say, 'I have not sinned.'"

17. It is too often claim erroneously that your righteousness earned you victory, success, breakthrough, etc. Deuteronomy 9:4 says that it is not your righteousness that makes him drive away evil nations and enables you to possess the land of the heathen. Rather, it is because of their wickedness that God drove them out and dispossessed them of their lands for you.

    Deuteronomy 9:4

    "Do not think in your heart, after the LORD your God has cast them out before you, saying, 'Because of my righteousness the LORD has brought me in to possess this land'; but *it is* because of the wickedness of these nations *that* the LORD is driving them out from before you."

18. It is to lift your heart and claim to be a god (Ezekiel 28:2).

    Ezekiel 28:2

    "Son of man, say to the prince of Tyre, 'Thus says the Lord GOD: "Because your heart *is* lifted up, And you say, 'I *am* a god, I sit *in* the seat of gods, In the midst of the seas,' Yet you *are* a man, and not a god, Though you set your heart as the heart of a god."

19. It is to say that you have fellowship with God and yet walk in darkness. The self-righteous lie and do not practice the truth (1 John 1:5-6).

    1 John 1:5-6

    This is the message which we have heard from Him and declare to you, that God is light and in Him is no darkness at all. If we say that we have fellowship with Him, and walk in darkness, we lie and do not practice the truth.

20. It is to claim to be pure in your own eyes, yet not washed from your filthiness (Proverbs 30:12).

Proverbs 30:12

"There is a generation that is pure in its own eyes,
Yet is not washed from its filthiness."

21. It is to have a heart that is weak and desperately wicked (Jeremiah 17:9).

Jeremiah 17:9

"The heart *is* deceitful above all *things,*
And desperately wicked; Who can know it?"

22. It is to neglect the weightier matters like justice, mercy, and faithfulness. The self-righteous are blind guides who strain out a gnat and swallow a camel! (Matthew 23:23-24),

Matthew 23:23-24

"Woe to you, scribes and Pharisees, hypocrites! For you pay tithe of mint and anise and cummin, and have neglected the weightier *matters* of the law: justice and mercy and faith. These you ought to have done, without leaving the others undone. Blind guides, who strain out a gnat and swallow a camel!"

23. It is to justify yourself in the sight of men, but God knows your heart, for that which is esteemed among men is detestable in the sight of God (Luke 16:15).

Luke 16:15

"And He said to them, "You are those who justify yourselves before men, but God knows your hearts. For what is highly esteemed among men is an abomination in the sight of God."

24. It is to be gardened by the deceitfulness of sin (Hebrews 3:13).

Hebrews 3:13

"but exhort one another daily, while it is called "Today," lest any of you be hardened through the deceitfulness of sin."

25. It is to trust in yourself that you are righteous and view others with contempt. This is revealed in the story of the Pharisee and the tax collector in Luke 18:9-11.

Luke 18:9-11

"Also He spoke this parable to some who trusted in themselves that they were righteous, and despised others: "Two men went up to the temple to pray, one a Pharisee and the other a tax collector. The Pharisee stood and prayed thus with himself, 'God, I thank You that I am not like other men—extortioners, unjust, adulterers, or even as this tax collector.""

26. It is to do things from selfishness or empty conceit and not regard others as more important as yourself (Philippians 2:3).

Philippians 2:3

"Let nothing be done through selfish ambition or conceit, but in lowliness of mind let each esteem others better than himself."

27. It is to commend yourself rather than allowing God to commend you (2 Corinthians 10:18).

Corinthians 10:18

"For not he who commends himself is approved, but whom the Lord commends."

28. It is to seek to be justified by law. Hence, the self-righteous person falls from grace and is severed from Christ Jesus (Galatians 5:4).

Galatians 5:4

"You have become estranged from Christ, you who attempt to be justified by law; you have fallen from grace."

29. It is to shift the blame and responsibility of your misdeed to others and seek excuses and justification (1 Samuel 15:13-21).

1 Samuel 15:13-21

Then Samuel went to Saul, and Saul said to him, "Blessed *are* you of the LORD! I have performed the commandment of the LORD." But Samuel said, "What then *is* this bleating of the sheep in my ears, and the lowing of the oxen which I hear?" And Saul said, "They have brought them from the Amalekites; for the people spared the best of the sheep and the oxen, to sacrifice to the LORD your God; and the rest we have utterly destroyed." Then Samuel said to Saul, "Be quiet! And I will tell you what the LORD said to me last night." And he said to him, "Speak on." So Samuel said, "When you *were* little in your own eyes, *were* you not head of the tribes of Israel? And did not the LORD anoint you king over Israel? Now the LORD sent you on a mission, and said, 'Go, and utterly destroy the sinners, the Amalekites, and fight against them until they are consumed.' Why then did you not obey the voice of the LORD? Why did you swoop down on the spoil, and do evil in the sight of the LORD?" And Saul said to Samuel, "But I have obeyed the voice of the LORD, and gone on the mission on which the LORD sent me, and brought back Agag king of Amalek; I have utterly destroyed the Amalekites. But the people took of the plunder, sheep and oxen, the best of the things which should have been utterly destroyed, to sacrifice to the LORD your God in Gilgal."

30. It is to deny your sinful state and need for salvation. The self-righteous say they have not sinned. They make God a liar and His word is not in them (1 John 1:10).

1 John 1:10

"If we say that we have not sinned, we make Him a liar, and His word is not in us."

31. It is to live in self-deceit. The self-righteous are those who are blind but claim that they can see. Hence, they could not avail themselves of the blessings of God (John 9:39-41).

John 9:39-41

"And Jesus said, "For judgment I have come into this world, that those who do not see may see, and that those who see may be made blind." Then *some* of the Pharisees who were with Him heard these words, and said to Him, "Are we blind also?" Jesus said to them, "If you were blind, you would have no sin; but now you say, 'We see.' Therefore your sin remains."

32. It is to say that you are rich and have become wealthy and have need of nothing. The self-righteous do not know that they are according to the scriptures wretched, miserable, poor, blind, and naked.

33. It is to have confidence in your own righteousness. It is to seek to save yourself through works. It is a rejection of Jesus.

34. It is not having right standing with God and seeking to have right living with man.

35. It is to justify yourself by blaming others. Self-righteousness is a very difficult sin to get people to see and condemn in themselves. It is a terrible sin because it keeps people from seeing their need for the gospel. It believes in the lie that we can be good enough in ourselves to qualify for heaven.

It makes us believe that we do not need a Saviour who died on the Cross to pay the penalty for our sins. It makes us speak and act with the air of "I am not like the worst sinners who need a Saviour and God would not judge a good person like me." (1 Timothy 1:15-17). Paul enjoined people to repent of self-righteous hypocrisy and stop storing up wrath for the day of judgment. It is wrong to judge others and secretly engage in the same behavior that you openly condemn.

THE CHARACTER OF A SELF-RIGHTEOUS PERSON

A self-righteous person is defined as one who is confident in his or her own righteousness. A self-righteous person also exhibits superiority toward everyone else, particularly if that other person holds a different opinion.

Self-righteousness is a fatal sin! It attracts God's wrath and judgment. It is difficult to detect for many people. Several self-righteous people do not agree that they are guilty of self-righteousness. Self-righteousness and pride are cousins. They birth self-righteous attitudes and have drastic tragic consequences. Proverbs 21:2 says, "Every way of a man is right in his own eyes: but the LORD pondereth the hearts."

A person full of self-righteousness...

1. Is arrogant before God and is rejected (Luke 18:11)
2. Tries to rely on self-justification (Luke 10:29; 16:15)
3. Rejects the justice that comes from God (Rom. 10:3)
4. Condemns those who are truly righteous (Matt. 9:11-13; Luke 7:39)
5. Considers himself righteous before his own eyes (Prov. 21:2).
6. Takes pride in his own works (Prov. 20:6)
7. Is disapproved before God's eyes (Isa. 65:5).

The following are more important traits that define a self-righteous person:

1. Self-righteous people think of themselves as being important: Some preachers brag about their sermons and some Lay Christians brag about how good they are. I know a Christian Brother who frequently talks about how many times he fasts per week and how many hours he spends in prayer daily, especially in speaking in tongues. He believes that this makes him more righteous and more spiritual than other Christians around him. The irony of it is that the Brother does not pay tithe and insists that the New Testament does not teach the payment of tithe.

There is a difference between being self-right and being Christ right. Self-righteousness means being self-right. It is to focus on self or to be self-centered. When we allow this attitude to dominate our lives, we begin to think and say that without us our church cannot grow in population and spiritual matters. We begin to hype our achievements and say that our sermons are the best in the world, pride ourselves on the number of souls we have won for Christ, how much we pay as tithe, and so on. God wants us to be Christ-right and Christ-focused.

Sometimes we think so highly of ourselves that we felt that God needs us so badly. Actually, the reverse is true: It is us that desperately needs God! Righteous people follow Jesus and consider the things that show God's grace and mercy. Self-righteous people focus on how good and strong they are in comparison to other people. The scripture in 2 Corinthians 10:12 says "For we dare not class ourselves or compare ourselves with those who commend themselves. But they, measuring themselves by themselves, and comparing themselves among themselves, are not wise."

2. Self-righteous people like to be praised for their works: If we are His servants, we are called to take up our cross and glorify Him by daily dying to our old selves and walking in the newness of life that we have been given in Christ. Matthew 16:24-27 affirms this, "Then said Jesus unto his disciples, If any man will come after me, let him deny himself, and take up his cross, and follow me. For whosoever will save his life shall lose it: and whosoever will lose his life for my sake shall find it. For what is a man profited, if he shall gain the whole world, and lose his own soul? or what shall a man give in exchange for his soul? For the Son of man shall come in the glory of his Father with his angels, and then he shall reward every man according to his works."

Beloved, your righteous deeds are filthy rags. You deserve nothing, but Christ allows you to breathe. If you must boast, then boast about what Christ did for you on the cross. Only the righteousness that God gives can earn you abundant and eternal life. Your own righteousness cannot earn it for you. Galatians 6:14 says "But God forbid that I should boast except in the cross of our Lord Jesus Christ, by whom the world has been crucified to me, and I to the world."

3. Self-righteous people justify themselves before God: We must be careful not to justify our sins. If God's word says it is a sin, it is a sin. We must be careful that we do not treat God as though He owes us a pat on the back because of what we see as our goodness. God's eternal truth is that all have sinned and have come short of the glory of God. Therefore, only God can qualify you and me for the best things in life and eternity. In 2 Corinthians 10:17-18 affirms "But "he who glories, let him glory in the Lord." For not he who commends himself is approved, but whom the Lord commends."

    Like Job, we may talk back to God and rationalize our thoughts and actions. We may show God how rich, how we have increased in goods, and how we have need of nothing (Revelation 3:17). We may tell God how good we are by following His commandments and that He owes us a pat on the back and praises! However, just like the Laodicean church, we didn't know that we are actually "wretched, miserable, and poor, and blind, and naked" (same verse).

    Revelation 3:17 says "You say, 'I am rich; I have acquired wealth and do not need a thing.' But you do not realize that you are wretched, pitiful, poor, blind, and naked."

4. Self-righteous people are always ready to share a list of their good works: It is not our responsibility to keep a record of our good works. The scripture teaches us that God is not unrighteous to forget our work and labor of love that we have shown forth in HIS name. 1 Corinthians 13:3 affirms this truth "And though I bestow all my goods to feed *the poor*, and though I give my body to be burned, but have not love, it profits me nothing."

5. Self-righteous people condemn sinners: The danger of being self-righteous is that we think we are in the position of God. However, God did not even send His Son into the world to condemn the world, but to save the world through Him (John 3:17). Truly, righteous people love the sinner but hate the sin. When we love the sinner, it does not mean that we approve of his or her sin, but we love the sinner because we are like "God who is Love". Even Christians must keep in mind that we all

have sinned, and we still fall short of doing things that bring God glory. We glory in God who gives us victory. 1 John 5:4-6 says "For whatever is born of God overcomes the world. And this is the victory that has overcome the world—our faith. Who is he who overcomes the world, but he who believes that Jesus is the Son of God?"

6. Self-righteous people repel others: it is not difficult to identify self-righteous people. They make you feel uncomfortable, unrighteous, and guilty because you can see how they obviously rub their righteous acts on your face and, in the process, unconsciously put you down or weaken your self-worth and faith. As a result, you do not like to make friends with these people because of their aura of making you feel spiritually inferior. That is exactly what self-righteousness does. It repels people. On the other hand, genuine righteousness draws people toward you. Jesus Christ is the perfect example of a righteous Being. He draws people toward Him and does not repel them.

7. Self-righteous people parade their good works: The Pharisees and scribes are the perfect examples of self-righteousness. For that reason, Christ ardently reprimanded them. On many occasions in Matthew 23, Christ said, "Woe to you, Scribes and Pharisees." Similarly, in Matthew 5:20, Jesus Christ stated that we must exceed the righteousness of these people if ever we want to enter the Kingdom of God.

   What makes the Pharisees and Scribes self-righteous and deserving of Christ's reprimand? First, they love to publicly display their righteousness to people. They were "wearing their righteousness outwardly." When they fast, they want to appear to people fasting (Matthew 6:16). When they repent, they do not produce the fruit of repentance (Matthew 3:8). When they give alms, they sound a trumpet and announce their good acts (Matthew 6:2). And the list just goes on and on. That is why we often say that self-righteousness is more of an outward manifestation rather than an inward conversion of the person

8. Self-righteous people are uncompassionate: Our righteous Jesus demonstrated genuine compassion to people on many occasions. In

Luke 7, he showed compassion to the widow of Nain and raised her son to life. Similarly, when he saw that the people that came to hear his teaching were hungry, the Bible says that he saw them as sheep without shepherds and had compassion on them. Thereafter, he multiplied the five loaves of bread and two pieces of fish and fed the 5000 people with them. However, being self-righteous makes you a person without much compassion. Why? Because you see other people full of sins and faults and you do not understand why they are that way. You have a hard time looking into yourself and realizing that you also have a lot of unchecked problems. Instead of being compassionate, self-righteous people are very critical of others.

JESUS HEALED THE MAN WITH A
WITHERED HAND - MARK 3:1-6

And He entered the synagogue again, and a man was there who had a withered hand. So they watched Him closely, whether He would heal him on the Sabbath, so that they might accuse Him. And He said to the man who had the withered hand, "Step forward." Then He said to them, "Is it lawful on the Sabbath to do good or to do evil, to save life or to kill?" But they kept silent. And when He had looked around at them with anger, being grieved by the hardness of their hearts, He said to the man, "Stretch out your hand." And he stretched it out, and his hand was restored as whole as the other. Then the Pharisees went out and immediately plotted with the Herodians against Him, how they might destroy Him."

9. Self-righteous people hate and condemn sinners: As righteous persons, God expects us to hate sin and love sinners. On the contrary, a self-righteous person hates sinners instead of just hating their sins. When self-righteous people come in contact with adulterers, thieves, extortionists, or somebody who has committed a terrible crime or horrible sin, they would hate, castigate, and condemn the sinful. Jesus Christ loves sinners. He even ate with tax collectors and talked to them. He spent more time with the perceived sinful people in His earth walk than the Pharisees who are thought to be "righteous." Self-righteousness makes

people believe that they are in the position of God. They condemn people and pass permanent judgment. They determine who will be part of God's kingdom and who will not.

10. Self-righteous people love the approval and praises of men: In Matthew 5:16, the Bible says that we should do our good deeds so that people "may see [our] good works and glorify [our] Father in heaven." Beloved, when you do something good, you do it not to show how righteous you are, But instead, you do it to demonstrate the majesty of the loving God. Often, a self-righteous person wants to gain approval from people. He wants to look righteous, so people hold him in high regard. The Pharisees are exactly like that. They did their alms in front of many people, disfigured their faces when fasting, loved to sit at the best seats in the synagogues, give alms with a lot of show-off, and enjoyed being called pompous titles, just to name a few. Unfortunately, they have their rewards. They will miss out on the greater reward that only God can give them.

11. Self-righteous people list their good works: Do you belong to the category of Christians who keep a mental note of their good deeds and announce them to everyone to prove that they are righteous? You must pray against self-righteousness. When we do this, we forget that our righteousness is just like FILTHY RAGS (Isaiah 64:6). Our righteousness pales down to nothing when compared to the righteousness of God. The truth is that it is not our job to list our good deeds. It is God's. "For God is not unrighteous to forget [our] work and labor of love, which [we] have showed towards his name, in that [we] have ministered to the saints and do minister" (Hebrews 6:10).

12. Self-righteous people reject correction: Righteousness makes a Christian teachable and humble. Self-righteousness, on the other hand, will make anyone proud, unteachable, and callous. The hardness of the heart may spring from the belief that you know almost everything, that you already know what the scripture says, and nothing new can impress you anymore. It also makes you think that there is nothing to learn anymore, and you will not let anybody tell you what to do. You will become so vain in your thinking that you will not allow anyone to

point out where you might have got it wrong. Beloved, God wants you to demonstrate a child-like attitude. Jesus Christ was teachable in spite of His wisdom and divine nature. He did everything and anything His Father told Him to do. I enjoin you to make Him your perfect example.

13. Self-righteous people wallow in self-pity: Every time a self-righteous is chastened by God, he sulks in self-pity. Instead of seeing trials and challenges in life as a way to develop godly righteousness, they would instead pity and prevent themselves from developing the enthusiasm to fight back. James said that we must "count it all joy when [we] fall into various trials." For a self-righteous person, would just endure the trial and not actually rejoice in it. WE NEED TO SEE CORRECTION AS A WAY TO BRING US BACK TO OUR LOVING FATHER. When God permits a trial, it is NOT because He wants to prevent us from getting into the Kingdom, but to help us develop the righteousness that enables us to be part of His family.

When we are corrected for our self-righteous arrogance, we must have a positive attitude, learn the lesson, and overcome. That's the only way we can destroy the shackles of self-righteousness that restrict our spiritual growth.

And self-righteous people who believe they're getting to heaven by being good enough – or people like those Jesus described in Luke 18:9 [who] trust in themselves that they are righteous – are shooting at the wrong target. Romans 10:3 says, "They being ignorant of God's righteousness, and SEEKING TO ESTABLISH THEIR OWN RIGHTEOUSNESS, have not submitted to the righteousness of God." To the Christians, 2 Corinthians 13:5 tells us to "Examine yourselves to see whether you are in the faith; test yourselves. Do you not realize that Christ Jesus is in you? Unless you do, of course, you will fail the test.

"Examine yourselves as to whether you are in the faith. Test yourselves. Do you not know yourselves, that Jesus Christ is in you?—unless indeed you are disqualified."

- Corinthians 13:5

TWO

CAUSES OF SELF-RIGHTEOUSNESS

Self-righteousness is one of the by-products of the fall of man and his carnal or Adamic nature. Adam and Eve fell because they allowed the enemy to deceive them into focusing on themselves rather than on God. This singular act ruined their intimacy with God, stole the dominion they enjoyed, and cut them from fully enjoying the God-kind-of-life (Zoe). Similarly, when the self is introduced or added to self-righteousness, it ruins the whole essence of righteousness and produces sin and judgment rather than Divine approval and immense rewards. In the preceding chapter, we clearly stated that God detests and punishes self-righteousness because it does not bring honor and glory to Him. We also enumerated the signs of self-righteousness as well as the characters of self-righteous people.

In this chapter, we shall examine the causes of self-righteousness. By so doing, we shall successfully avoid falling into the trap of self-righteousness or pray ourselves out, if we find ourselves entangled by it.

Self-righteousness is ungodly and detestable to God. It also attracts serious consequences. Therefore, the first step towards overcoming it is to proactively learn its causes and avoid it like a plague, with prayer and the help of the Blessed Holy Spirit.

1. Excessive Focus on Self: The only true source of righteousness is God. No one else can give you righteousness or make you righteous. You

cannot make yourself righteous either, no matter what you do in terms of good works or deeds. You cannot earn righteousness; it is God's gift to His children. Therefore, the spirit and attitude of self-righteousness springs from the erroneous belief that you have righteousness of your own or that you can make yourself righteous. The power and grace for you to live right with man and stand right with God can only be conferred on you by God. It is not by might nor by power, but by His Spirit (Zechariah 4:6). When you attempt to become righteous by your own efforts or declare that you are righteous, using your own criteria rather than God's, you become guilty of self-righteousness and give its spirit free course to operate in your life.

Often, we think that we are better than anyone because we have done a lot of good things. We think others are less important or have no good work. We have the self-delusion that we are so good, and that God needs us. We deceive ourselves by believing we do not need a Savior and that we are spiritually healthy on our own. This is where and how self-righteousness starts. The thoughts become actions and the actions give birth to the attitudes and sins of self-righteousness. The position of the Bible is that believers should let God take all the glory and honor in all they do. God will not share His glory with anyone. The greatest sin that emanates from self is that of usurping or taking the glory that belongs to God. In Matthew 5:16, the Bible says," Let your light so shine that men will see your good works and glorify your Father who is in heaven.

I would like you to note that the Bible did not say that when you do good works and men know about it, they should give glory to you. No, the gory does not belong to you. Don't seek it and don't demand it or encourage men to give it to you. It belongs to God and should be given to Him. All believers must be careful and not allow pride to lead them to sin against God. They also need to exercise caution and resist the sin to lead others astray from God.

God will accept the humble and the contrite, but He puts far from Him those who glory in themselves. Indeed, my brethren, what have we to glory in? Is not every boast a lie? What is this self-hood but a peacock feather, fit only for the cap of a fool? May God deliver us from exalting self; and yet we cannot be delivered from so doing if we hold in any degree the doctrine of salvation by our own good works.

2. Ignorance: This is another cause of self-righteousness. The Bible says that my people are destroyed because of a lack of knowledge (Hosea 4:6). Many do not know the truth; hence, they are not free from the prison of ignorance and are being ruined by its consequences. People who seek self-justification and self-righteousness do so because they are either ignorant of the truth or have refused to accept the truth that the sacrificial, atoning, finished, complete, and perfect work of Jesus Christ on the Cross at Calvary, as well as His shed blood, earned for all sinners salvation and eternal life. The sinner, on his or her own, cannot earn it as a reward for his or he works. It is the gift of God that every man must receive by faith to be saved. The ignorance of this truth is a major cause of self-righteousness. This also points to the need to ensure that wrong teachings and doctrines are discouraged in the Church and that wrong teachers are exposed and corrected. Teachings that encourage self-righteousness are injurious to the gospel and the Church. They must be stopped and uprooted. Jesus said that every tree my heavenly Father has not planted shall be uprooted.

The self-righteous believe that the blood of Jesus which was shed for us at Calvary is not price enough as atonement for our sins till man adds his silver or his gold or his works. The implication of this is that the self-righteous erroneously and ignorantly believe that Christ's blood is not our redemption at all, and Christ is no Redeemer. What an error born out of ignorance! To conclude, as the self-righteous person does, that our Lord's bearing of sin for us did not make a perfect atonement and that it is ineffectual till we either do or suffer something to complete it, then in the supplemental work lies the real value, and Christ's work is on itself insufficient. If one believes in Christ is not completely saved by what Jesus has done, but must do something himself to complete it, then salvation was not finished, and the Savior's work remains imperfect till we poor sinners lend a hand to make up for His deficiencies. Ignorance makes people believe in a lie and suffer needless pain.

Also due to monumental ignorance of the self-righteous, he or she rejects the covenant which was sealed with Christ's death. If we can be saved by the old covenant of works, then the new covenant was not required. The sacrifice of Jesus ratified the new covenant. No one ever was saved under the old covenant of works, nor ever will be, and the new covenant is introduced for that reason. The spirit of self-righteousness, which holds that a man can be saved by his own good works, pours contempt upon the testament of love that the death of Jesus has put in force.

The ignorance or error that man can earn justification, righteousness, salvation, and eternal life through His works is the bane of the religions of the world today. The consequence of this error and ignorance is that it hinders the victims from receiving by faith the salvation and righteousness that God gives by grace and free to His children. Paul was not ignorant of this great truth. He condemned self-righteousness and taught believers not to allow its spirit to reign in their lives or rule over them. In Galatians 2:21, the distinguished apostle said, "I do not frustrate the grace of God: for if righteousness comes by the law, then Christ is dead in vain." They are also in great ignorance concerning themselves, for those very persons who are self-righteousness, they are as a rule openly chargeable with a fault; and if not, were they to sit down and look at their own lives, they would soon perceive an event in their best works such impurity of motive beforehand, or such pride and self-congratulation afterward, that they would see the gloss taken off from all their performances, and they would be utterly ashamed of them. Nor is it ignorance alone which leads men to self-righteousness, they are also deceived by pride."

3. Pride: The Bible affirms that God hates pride and that every one that is proud is an abomination to Him (Proverbs 6:5, 16-17). God expects us to hate pride too. Proverbs 8:13 says "The fear of the Lord *is* to hate evil; Pride and arrogance and the evil way and the perverse mouth I hate." Pride, a bedfellow to self-righteousness, is a sin and not a virtue. 1 John 2:16 affirms that pride is not of the Father but of the world. Proverbs 21:4 states that "A haughty look, a proud heart, *And* the plowing of the wicked *are* sin."

22

It is wrong for us to be proud and self-righteous because the Lord is the greatest of the greatest; we are not. The following Scriptures underscore this very important point:

Psalm 65:5-7

By terrible things in righteousness wilt thou answer us, O God of our salvation; who art the confidence of all the ends of the earth, and of them that are afar off upon the sea: Which by his strength setteth fast the mountains; being girded with power: Which stilleth the noise of the seas, the noise of their waves, and the tumult of the people.

Psalm 97:9

For thou, Lord, art high above all the earth: thou art exalted far above all gods.

Philippians 29-10

Wherefore God also hath highly exalted him and given him a name which is above every name: That at the name of Jesus, every knee should bow, of things in heaven, and things in earth, and things under the earth.

Also, it is wrong for us to be proud and self-righteous because God alone should get the glory.

1 Corinthians 10:31

Whether therefore ye eat, or drink, or whatsoever ye do, do all to the glory of God.

Jeremiah 9:23-24

Thus saith the Lord, Let not the wise man glory in his wisdom, neither let the mighty man glory in his might, let not the rich man glory in his riches: But let him that glorieth glory in this, that he understandeth and knoweth me, that I am the Lord which exercises loving kindness, judgment, and righteousness, in the earth: for in these things I delight, saith the Lord.

1 Corinthians 1: 28-29

And base things of the world, and things which are despised, hath God chosen, yea, and things which are not, to bring to nought things that are: That no flesh should glory in his presence.

Pride and self-righteousness are the reasons many people are guilty of robbing God of the glory that belongs exclusively to Him.

PRIDE AND SELF-RIGHTEOUSNESS MAKE US IGNORE AND FORGET GOD

Deuteronomy 8:14

Then thine heart be lifted up, and thou forget the Lord thy God, which brought thee forth out of the land of Egypt, from the house of bondage;

Psalm 10:4

The wicked, through the pride of his countenance, will not seek after God: God is not in all his thoughts.

Hosea 13:6b

According to their pasture, so were they filled; they were filled, and their heart was exalted; therefore have they forgotten me.

PRIDE AND SELF-RIGHTEOUSNESS MAKE US TO REBEL AGAINST THE WORD OF GOD

The word of God is supposed to be the believer's final authority and compass, but when we decide to seek our own way to righteousness, salvation, and eternal life outside God's word, we become guilty of these twin evils pride and self-righteousness. We also offend God greatly.

Nehemiah 9:16, 17, 29

But they and our fathers dealt proudly, and hardened their necks, and hearkened not to thy commandments... And refused to obey, neither were mindful of thy wonders that thou didst among them; but hardened their necks, and in their rebellion appointed a captain to return to their bondage: but thou art a God ready to pardon, gracious and merciful, slow to anger, and of great kindness, and forsookest them not... and testifiedst against them, that thou mightest bring them again unto thy law: yet they dealt proudly, and hearkened not unto thy commandments, but sinned against thy judgments, (which if a man do, he shall live in them;) and withdrew the shoulder, and hardened their neck, and would not hear.

PRIDE AND SELF-RIGHTEOUSNESS GIVE US AN EXAGGERATED SENSE OF GREATNESS

Obadiah 3

The pride of thine heart hath deceived thee, thou that dwellest in the clefts of the rock, whose habitation is high; that saith in his heart, Who shall bring me down to the ground?

Romans 12:3

For I say, through the grace given unto me, to every man that is among you, not to think of himself more highly than he ought to think, but to think soberly, according as God hath dealt to every man the measure of faith.

Galatians 6:3

For if a man think himself to be something, when he is nothing, he deceiveth himself.

PRIDE AND SELF-RIGHTEOUSNESS CREATE SELF-EXALTATION AND A DESIRE TO BE HONOURED

The Scriptures provide several passages to corroborate this point:

Proverbs 25:27

It is not good to eat much honey: so for men to search their own glory is not glory.

Matthew 23:5-7

But all their works they do for to be seen of men: they make broad their phylacteries, and enlarge the borders of their garments, And love the uppermost rooms at feasts, and the chief seats in the synagogues, And greetings in the markets, and to be called of men, Rabbi, Rabbi.

Mark 12:38-39

And he said unto them in his doctrine, Beware of the scribes, which love to go in long clothing, and love salutations in the marketplaces, And the chief seats in the synagogues, and the uppermost rooms at feasts:

Jude 16

These are murmurers, complainers, walking after their own lusts; and their mouth speaketh great swelling words, having men's persons in admiration because of advantage.

A self-righteous person who prays draws attention to himself rather than God. God must shudder when He witnesses the feeble attempt of a self-righteous prayer. It leaves the lips of the self-righteous and falls to the ground, never making it to Christ for His consideration. Pride pulls prayer back down to earth. Prideful praying is ineffective and unacceptable to God.

Can pride really engulf a praying person? Unfortunately, it absolutely can. This is why God must root out pride in our lives on a regular basis. Pride never goes away. Pride lusts after God's job. Pride is not content in the role of a humble, submitted, and obedient follower of Christ. Pride puts others down to build up its own ego. Humility, in contrast, is quick to build others up and bridge them to God. The humble are quick to confess their sins and shortcomings. Unfortunately, the proud and self-righteous are not!

Pride and self-righteousness will make us to seek to please men rather than God. In the end, we displease God and attract His judgment (1 Samuel 15:30; John 12:43; Galatians 1:10).

Pride and self-righteousness make us think we are "wise". The Bible warns us sternly against this. Proverbs 3:7 admonishes, "Be not wise in thine own eyes: fear the Lord." 1 Corinthians 3:18 says, "Let no man deceive himself. If any … seemeth wise." 1 Corinthians 8:2 adds, "If any think he knoweth anything, he knoweth nothing yet as he ought to know." Pride and self-righteousness give us a "know-it-all" attitude (Psalm 131:1; Proverbs 26:12).

Pride and self-righteousness corrupt us (Mark 7:22-23). It also brings about the downfall of its victim (Proverbs 11:2a; Proverbs 16:18; Proverbs 18:12a; Proverbs 29:23a; Ezekiel 28:12-17; Isaiah 14:12-15; Daniel 5:18, 20, 21 and 1 Corinthians 10:12). Beloved, you should avoid pride and self-righteousness like a plague.

4. Unbelief: Self-righteousness also arises from wicked unbelief, for through his self-conceit man will not believe God. Nothing is more plainly revealed in Scripture than this, that by the works of the law shall no man be justified, yet men in some shape or other stick to the hope of legal righteousness; they will have it that they must prepare for grace, or assist mercy, or in some degree deserve eternal life. They prefer their own flattering prejudices to the declaration of the heart-searching God. They desire to have a finger in their own salvation and claim at least a little credit for it.

The testimony of the Holy Spirit concerning the deceitfulness of the heart is put aside, and the declaration of God that there is none that doeth good, no, not one, is altogether denied. This is a great evil and should be avoided!

Unbelief is a major hindrance and destroyer, as far as Christianity is concerned. Without faith, it is impossible to please God. (Hebrews 11:6). Therefore, unbelief makes you displease God. Self-righteousness is a clear declaration of a lack of belief in God's word and position that righteousness and salvation come not by the sinner's work but by the atoning sacrifice of His Son, Jesus Christ, the Savior, and Redeemer of the whole world.

Failure to believe that this finished work of Jesus is truly finished, complete and perfect and that it has accomplished the salvation of mankind, and that is freely given by grace and is to be claimed by faith is an insult to heaven.

5.   Frustrating the grace of God: In Galatians 2:21, Apostle Paul, speaking by the Holy Ghost said, "I do not frustrate the grace of God: for if righteousness comes by the law, then Christ is dead in vain."

One of the chief misdeeds of a self-righteous person is that he or she frustrates the grace of God. What does it mean to "frustrate" the grace of God? It is to receive grace but not be gracious. It is to continue to look at things from your own point of view. It is to remain a spiritual babe. It is to refuse to not share His grace with others.

Similarly, in Ephesians 2:8, the Bible says, "By grace are ye saved through faith; and that not of yourselves: it is the gift of God." More than that, he who trusts in himself, his feelings, his works, his prayers, or in anything except the grace of God, virtually gives up trusting in the grace of God altogether: for be it was known unto you, that God's grace will never share the work with man's merit. As oil will not combine with water, so neither will human merit and heavenly mercy mix together.

The apostle said in Romans 11:6, "If by grace, then it is no more of works; otherwise, grace is no more grace. But if it is of works, then is it no more grace: otherwise, work is no more work." You must either have salvation wholly because you deserve it, or wholly because God graciously bestows it though you do not deserve it. You must receive salvation at the Lord's hand either as a debt or as a charity; there can be no mingling of the ideas.

That which is a pure donation of favor cannot also be a reward of personal deserving. A combination of the two principles of law and grace is utterly impossible. Trust in our own works to any degree effectually shuts us out from all hope of salvation by grace, and so it frustrates the grace of God.

6. The natural superficiality of the human mind: Self-righteousness is also much promoted by the almost universal spirit of trifling which is now abroad. Only while men trifle with themselves can they entertain the idea of personal merit before God. He who comes to serious thought, and begins to understand the character of God, before whom the heavens are not pure, and the angels are charged with folly, he, I say, that comes to serious thought and beholds a true vision of God, abhors himself in dust and ashes, and is forever silenced as to any thought of self-justification.

When Prophet Isaiah, the son of Amoz, saw the Almighty God in His glory and splendor, he lost his attitude of self-righteousness and self-justification. He said, "Woe *is* me, for I am undone! Because I *am* a man of unclean lips, And I dwell in the midst of a people of unclean lips; For my eyes have seen the King, The LORD of hosts." (Isaiah 6:5). It takes a genuine encounter with God for anyone to be broken and to overcome the spirit of self-righteousness.

THREE

BIBLICAL EXAMPLES OF SELF-RIGHTEOUSNESS

There are Bible characters who exhibited the attitude of self-righteousness. In this chapter, we will turn the spotlight on these characters and learn a number of lessons from each of them. By so doing, we will be obeying God's words in 1 Corinthians 10:11 and Romans 15:4:

1 Corinthians 10:11

"Now all these things happened unto them for examples: and they are written for our admonition, upon whom the ends of the world are come."

Romans 15:4

"For whatsoever things were written aforetime were written for our learning, that we through patience and comfort of the scriptures might have hope."

TRYING TO LEGALISTICALLY KEEP THE LAW IS NOT GOD'S WILL

A. A legalist completely misses the main issue:

Matthew 15:2-6

"Why do thy disciples transgress the tradition of the elders? ... Ye transgress the commandment of God by your tradition."

Matthew 23:23-24

"For ye pay tithe of (spices) and have omitted the weightier (more important) matters of ... mercy, and faith ... Ye... strain at a gnat, and swallow a camel."

Mark 7:6-8

"Their heart is far from me... ye hold the tradition of men, (such) as the washing of pots and cups."

John 5:8-11

Jesus told a lame man, "Take up thy bed and walk." The legalists ignored the miraculous healing and told him it was not lawful to carry his bed on the Sabbath.

SATAN - OUR ORIGINAL ENEMY

Satan, the arch-enemy of mankind, was the first being to be filled with pride and self-righteous attitude. Therefore, the greatest example of self-righteousness in the Bible relates to satan or Lucifer, and how he went from being the greatest angel of God's army to being thrown out of heaven for mutiny against God. His pride and desire to be in control of heaven, based on his self-righteous attitude, led to him being rejected by God.

Ezekiel 28:14-15, 17

"Thou art the anointed cherub that covereth; and I have set thee so: thou wast upon the holy mountain of God; thou hast walked up and down in the midst of the stones of fire. Thou wast perfect in thy ways fro2m the day that thou wast created, till iniquity was found in thee. Thine heart was lifted up because of thy beauty, thou hast corrupted thy wisdom by reason of thy brightness: I will cast thee to the ground, I will lay thee before kings, that they may behold thee."

Isaiah 14:12-14 also says:

"How art thou fallen from heaven, O Lucifer, son of the morning! how art thou cut down to the ground, which didst weaken the nations! For thou hast said in thine heart, I will ascend into heaven, I will exalt my throne above the stars of God: I will sit also upon the mount of the congregation, in the sides of the north: I will ascend above the heights of the clouds; I will be like the most High."

The two passages above show that self-righteousness has been around from time immemorial. It began with satan. Its spirit and attitude have occupied the hearts of men.

As believers, we must be careful to examine ourselves from time to time and ensure that we are not self-righteous. Anytime we notice we are or someone draws our attention to it, we should quickly turn to God in prayer for help and repentance.

JOB

Job 32:1-2

Can you believe that the same Job who said to God, "Though you slay me, yet will I trust you", suffered from self-righteousness? In Job 32 we find that there was a friend of Job by the name of Elihu (the name means "He is my God"). He visited Job along with three other friends who had spent time falsely accusing Job. Job had defended himself over and over again.

Finally, these three friends stopped asking Job questions because they saw him as self-righteous. At this point, Elihu, who had been quiet, spoke up. He was angry with Job because Job justified himself rather than God. That is, Job gave himself credit for his goodness instead of God. He was angry with the other three friends because they had condemned Job without a cause.

Elihu said he had not spoken because he was younger and afraid to speak. However, he went on to say, "It is the spirit in a man, the breath of the Almighty, that gives understanding." Elihu did some profound teaching in chapters 32-37.

Then, in Job 38-41, we find the Lord speaking to Job about his behavior. When God finished speaking, Job humbles himself in chapter 42 and replies to God, "You asked, 'Who is this that obscures my counsel without knowledge. Surely, I spoke things I did not understand...'" Then, Job repented. (Job 42:1-6) and God blessed the latter part of Job's life more than the first.

It is difficult to detect self-righteousness in our own lives. It usually takes others, or the word of God, to point it out to us. We might even become a little angry if one of our peers points it out to us. Therefore, if Job could be self-righteous without knowing it initially, we need to be careful and watchful too, so we do not fall into the trap of self-righteousness. If we should become self-righteous, regardless of who or what points it out to us, we should take a lesson from Job and repent quickly.

NAAMAN

The truth that self-righteousness is a thief and that it has robbed men and women of things money cannot buy is exemplified in the story of Naaman, a commander in the Syrian army. The scripture says that he was a brave warrior, but he had leprosy. It means that he needed help with this health problem that was a sore spot in his life.

2 KINGS 5:2-3

"And the Syrians had gone out by companies and had brought away captive out of the land of Israel a little maid, and she waited on Naaman's wife. And she said unto her mistress, Would God my lord were with the prophet that is in Samaria! for he would recover him of his leprosy."

God uses the foolish things of the world to confound the wise and the base things to confound the put the powerful to shame. He sometimes provides help for us in unlikely places. Here, God chose to use a captive girl who is a maid to Naaman's wife as his destiny helper. He provided Naaman with the answer to what he needed. Through a series of events, after a letter had been written, Naaman comes to the prophet's house to meet him but is met there by a messenger.

In 2 Kings 5:10-14, the Bible says:

"And Elisha sent a messenger unto him, saying, Go and wash in Jordan seven times, and thy flesh shall come again to thee, and thou shalt be clean. But Naaman was wroth, and went away, and said, Behold, I thought, He will surely come out to me, and stand, and call on the name of the LORD his God, and strike his hand over the place, and recover the leper. Are not Abana and Pharpar, rivers of Damascus, better than all the waters of Israel? may I not wash in them, and be clean? So he turned and went away in a rage."

"And his servants came near, and spake unto him, and said, My father, if the prophet had bid thee do some great thing, wouldest thou not have done it? how much rather then, when he saith to thee, Wash, and be clean? Then went he down, and dipped himself seven times in Jordan, according to the saying of the man of God: and his flesh came again like unto the flesh of a little child, and he was clean."

Naaman almost didn't receive what he needed because of pride and a self-righteous attitude. He thought that because of his position, he deserves special treatment from the prophet. We see here that self-righteousness is a thief. It will rob you of what you need most. So beware of self-righteousness

THE RICH YOUNG RULER

While Naaman received by the grace and mercy of God, what he needed and escape from the evil agenda of the spirit of self-righteousness. The rich young ruler who had an encounter with Jesus Christ in Matthew 19:16-24 was not so favorable. His pride, presumption, and self-righteous attitude made him believe that he had what he needed. This robbed him of the eternal life that he so desperately needed. Jesus ultimately revealed to him that what he had was more important to him than what he said he needed.

Matthew 19:16-24

"And behold, one came and said unto him, Good Master, what good thing shall I do, that I may have eternal life? And he said unto him, Why callest thou me good? there is none good but one, that is, God: but if thou wilt enter into life, keep the commandments. He saith unto him, Which? Jesus said, Thou shalt do no murder, Thou shalt not commit adultery, Thou shalt not steal, Thou shalt not bear false witness, Honour thy father and thy mother: and Thou shalt love thy neighbor as thyself. The young man saith unto him, All these things have I kept from my youth up: what lack I yet? Jesus said unto him, If thou wilt be perfect, go and sell that thou hast, and give to the poor, and thou shalt have treasure in heaven: and come and follow me. But when the young man heard that saying, he went away sorrowful: for he had great possessions. Then said Jesus unto his disciples, Verily I say unto you, That a rich man shall hardly enter into the kingdom of heaven. And again I say unto you, It is easier for a camel to go through the eye of a needle, than for a rich man to enter into the kingdom of God."

The rich young man claimed to be righteous. So, he wanted to know what thing to do to guarantee eternal life. He thought that he could earn or inherit the kingdom through his works. Jesus asked him questions to find out how righteous the young rich man was and if he was living in obedience to the letter of the law only, or the spirit as well and to show him the true way of eternal life.

Although the man told Jesus that he had been obeying the law for a long time. Jesus made him know that he needed more than that and that God's grace was the essential requirement. When Jesus told him to sell all that he had and follow Him, the man became sad. He could not do so because he treasured his earthly possessions more than the heavenly hope. He chose to maintain his lifestyle than become a follower of Christ.

What did you learn in this encounter between Jesus and the young rich man? Self-righteousness robbed him of eternal life, the greatest need the man had, and the greatest blessing anyone on this side of eternity can have. I pray that you will not miss this blessing, in the name of Jesus.

THE PHARISES

The Pharisees were a perfect example of self-righteousness. The Bible attests to this on many occasions when Jesus Christ rebuked their attitudes of self-justification. For instance, Luke 18:9-14 contain the well-known parable of the Pharisee and the tax collector. Jesus told this parable to the religious leaders who TRUSTED IN THEMSELVES THAT THEY WERE RIGHTEOUS, and treated others with contempt:

Luke 10-14

"Two men went up into the temple to pray, one a Pharisee and the other a tax collector. The Pharisee, standing by himself, prayed thus: 'God, I thank you that I am not like other men, extortioners, unjust, adulterers, or even like this tax collector. I fast twice a week; I give tithes of all that I get."

The Pharisees were religious leaders. They have the 'I know it all attitude'. The Pharisee in this parable definitely thought he was spiritually healthy! Verse 9 says that these Pharisees or religious leaders **trusted in themselves that they were righteous.**

It is self-righteousness that makes people trust in their own righteousness at the expense of the righteousness they could have from Christ by faith.

In this parable, Jesus distinguished between a self-righteous attitude that leads to condemnation and divine punishment and humility or brokenness that leads to justification.

The Pharisees believed that his works were enough to make him earn him justification. That is why he confidently and pompously stood and prayed: "God, I thank you that I am not like other men, extortioners, unjust, adulterers, or even like this tax collector. I fast twice a week; I give tithes of all that I get." He saw himself as spiritually healthy and others as spiritually sick. He was a victim of monumental ignorance. He needed the Physician more but he did not know. Worse still, he did not know about the grace and mercy of God.

In Luke 18:13, we see a contrast to the Pharisee's self-righteous attitude in the prayer and actions of the tax collector. It says, "But the tax collector, standing far off, would not even lift up his eyes to heaven, but beat his breast, saying, 'God, be merciful to me, a sinner!" The next verse provides the result of Jesus' estimation of the two characters' attitudes: "I tell you, this man went down to his house justified, rather than the other. For everyone who exalts himself will be humbled, but the one who humbles himself will be exalted."

This verse again confirms that pride produces self-righteousness and that God detests and punishes it while humility wins His favor, blessings, and promotion. We see the sinner who looked the most unrighteous, justified or declared righteous, while the Pharisee was not.

The religious leaders show us that it is possible to think highly of ourselves while looking terribly at God. In fact, the more highly we think of ourselves, the worse we look to God. No one can be righteous or justified by works. Only God can confer righteousness and justification on us. Justification includes forgiveness and righteousness. It means that God has imputed or charged the guilt of our sin to His Son, Jesus Christ, and has imputed or credited Christ's righteousness to us. The antidote or cure to self-righteousness is humility.

If we study the teachings of Jesus in Matthew 23 (and other scriptures) we will find that Jesus condemned the self-righteousness of the Pharisees and Sadducees. They considered themselves righteous based on their own interpretation of their behavior and beliefs and not according to God. The word of God teaches us that we might think we're right in our own eyes but God looks at the heart.

Matthew 23:1-39

"Then spake Jesus to the multitude, and to his disciples, Saying The scribes and the Pharisees sit in Moses' seat: All therefore whatsoever they bid you observe, that observe and do; but do not ye after their works: for they say, and do not. For they bind heavy burdens and grievous to be borne, and lay them on men's shoulders; but they themselves will not move them with one of their fingers. But all their works they do for to be seen of men: they make broad their phylacteries, and enlarge the borders of their garments, And love the uppermost rooms at feasts, and the chief seats in the synagogues, And greetings in the markets, and to be called of men, Rabbi, Rabbi. But be not ye called Rabbi: for one is your Master, even Christ; and all ye are brethren. And call no man your father upon the earth: for one is your Father, which is in heaven. Neither be ye called masters: for one is your Master, even Christ. But he that is greatest among you shall be your servant. And whosoever shall exalt himself shall be abased; and he that shall humble himself shall be exalted. But woe unto you, scribes and Pharisees, hypocrites! for ye shut up the kingdom of heaven against men: for ye neither go in yourselves, neither suffer ye them that are entering to go in. Woe unto you, scribes and Pharisees, hypocrites! for ye devour widows' houses, and for a pretence make long prayer: therefore ye shall receive the greater damnation. Woe unto you, scribes and Pharisees, hypocrites! for ye compass sea and land to make one proselyte, and when he is made, ye make him twofold more the child of hell than yourselves. Woe unto you, ye blind guides, which say, Whosoever shall swear by the temple, it is nothing; but whosoever shall swear by the gold of the temple, he is a debtor! Ye fools and blind: for whether is greater, the gold, or the temple that sanctifieth the gold? And, Whosoever shall swear by the altar, it is nothing; but whosoever sweareth by the gift that is upon it, he is guilty. Ye fools and blind: for whether is greater, the gift, or the altar that sanctifieth the gift? Whoso therefore shall swear by the altar, sweareth by it, and by all things thereon. And whoso shall swear by the temple, sweareth by it, and by him that dwelleth therein. And he that shall swear by heaven, sweareth by the throne of God, and by him that sitteth thereon. Woe unto you, scribes and Pharisees, hypocrites! for ye pay tithe of mint and anise and cummin, and have omitted the weightier matters of the law, judgment, mercy, and faith: these ought ye to have done, and not to leave the other undone. Ye blind guides, which strain at a gnat, and swallow a camel. Woe unto you, scribes and Pharisees, hypocrites! for ye make clean the outside of the cup and of the platter, but within they are full of extortion and excess. Thou blind Pharisee, cleanse first that which is within the cup and platter, that the outside of them may be clean also.

Woe unto you, scribes and Pharisees, hypocrites! for ye are like unto whited sepulchres, which indeed appear beautiful outward, but are within full of dead men's bones, and of all uncleanness. Even so, ye also outwardly appear righteous unto men, but within ye are full of hypocrisy and iniquity. Woe unto you, scribes and Pharisees, hypocrites! because ye build the tombs of the prophets and garnish the sepulchres of the righteous, And say, If we had been in the days of our fathers, we would not have been partakers with them in the blood of the prophets. Wherefore ye be witnesses unto yourselves, that ye are the children of them which killed the prophets. Fill ye up then the measure of your fathers.

Ye serpents, ye generation of vipers, how can ye escape the damnation of hell? Wherefore, behold, I send unto you prophets, and wise men, and scribes: and some of them ye shall kill and crucify; and some of them shall ye scourge in your synagogues, and persecute them from city to city: That upon you may come all the righteous blood shed upon the earth, from the blood of righteous Abel unto the blood of Zacharias son of Barachias, whom ye slew between the temple and the altar. Verily I say unto you, All these things shall come upon this generation. O Jerusalem, Jerusalem, thou that killest the prophets, and stonest them which are sent unto thee, how often would I have gathered thy children together, even as a hen gathereth her chickens under her wings, and ye would not! Behold, your house is left unto you desolate. For I say unto you, Ye shall not see me henceforth, till ye shall say, Blessed is he that cometh in the name of the Lord."

Commentaries on Matthew 23 Verses 1-4

> "Then spake Jesus to the multitude, and to his disciples,
> Saying The scribes and the Pharisees sit in Moses' seat: All

therefore whatsoever they bid you observe, that observe and do; but do not ye after their works: for they say, and do not. For they bind heavy burdens and grievous to be borne and lay them on men's shoulders; but they themselves will not move them with one of their fingers."

Jesus states that they "sit in Moses' seat", which is symbolic of the authority that a rabbi has to teach. In verse 3, it seems as though Jesus wants the people to recognize their authority, and to "obey them and do everything they tell you", but he warns them not to do as they do. Here, Jesus makes acknowledgment that the leaders have the authority and the ability to interpret the Torah, but the example that the leaders set does not follow their teachings. In verse 4 Jesus speaks about the leaders and how they "tie up heavy loads and put them on men's shoulders, but they themselves are not willing to lift a finger to move them". This deals with how the leaders would not help out those people that were burdened with the rules they enforced. It is important to realize that Jesus is not saying that the leaders did not follow the rules themselves, just that they refused to help those weighed down by them. This way of acting is contradictory to Jesus as seen in Matthew 11:28-30 which says, "Come to me, all you who are weary and burdened, and I will give you rest. Take my yoke upon you and learn from me, for I am gentle and humble in heart, and you will find rest for your souls. for my yoke is easy and my burden is light."

Verses 5-7

"But all their works they do for to be seen of men: they make broad their phylacteries, and enlarge the borders of their garments, And love the uppermost rooms at feasts, and the chief seats in the synagogues And greetings in the markets, and to be called of men, Rabbi, Rabbi."

In verse 5, Jesus says that the Pharisees and leaders do things so that other men will see them. That is, they love to gain praise from others. It says that "they make their phylacteries wide and the tassels on their garments long". Phylacteries are small cases or boxes that contain slips on which passages were written. The passages used were Exodus 13:3-10, 11-16 (as remembrance of the deliverance of Israel from Egypt and the start of the

Passover), Deut. 6:4-9, and Deut. 11:13-21. These phylacteries were attached with straps to the forehead and left arm as reminders to follow God's law. In widening these straps and the tassels of their garments, the Pharisees and leaders stood out and they looked as if they followed the laws very well and were devout men. In verse 6, Jesus says that they love the places of honor and the most important seats, where one could be seen by all. As verse 7 says, they loved to be greeted and to be called 'Rabbi', which in Hebrew mean "my lord". The Pharisees and leaders demanded respect everywhere they went and thought of themselves as prestigious individuals.

Verses 8-12

"But be not ye called Rabbi: for one is your Master, even Christ; and all ye are brethren. And call no man your father upon the earth: for one is your Father, which is in heaven. Neither be ye called masters: for one is your Master, even Christ. But he that is greatest among you shall be your servant. And whosoever shall exalt himself shall be abased; a, and that shall humble himself shall be exalted."

In verses 8-11, we find Jesus saying that it is wrong for the Pharisees and teachers of the law from trying to be honored by having the term "Rabbi" as a title. He prohibits the term "Rabbi" from being used for the leaders, for there is only on "Master" (or Lord), and "you are all brothers", meaning that they are all equals. The term "father", which was also sometimes used in recognition of a teacher of the law, was also not to be used, as there is only one "Father" (God), as well as the title "teacher" for Christ, is the one true Teacher.

Verses 13-32: The Seven Woes

The 1st woe (v. 13): "But woe unto you, scribes and Pharisees, hypocrites! for ye shut up the kingdom of heaven against men: for ye neither go in yourselves, neither suffer ye them that are entering to go in."

Here, Jesus tells the teacher and Pharisees that they "shut the kingdom of heaven in men's faces." The "kingdom of heaven" is often thought of being the Gospel of Christ and the teachings of Jesus. Not only do the Pharisees not accept this, but they also prevent the people from acquiring this knowledge. There is a conflict between the traditional laws of Jewish leadership and the movement that comes along with Jesus.

The 2nd woe (v. 15): "Woe unto you, scribes and Pharisees, hypocrites! for ye compass sea and land to make one proselyte, and when he is made, ye make him twofold more the child of hell than yourselves."

Verse 15 refers to how hard the Pharisees would try to win a Gentile convert and make them into a proselyte. A proselyte was a pagan convert who was very zealous for the law. These converts that the Pharisees won were referred to as sons of hell because they were hostile towards the followers of Jesus who were less attentive to the law.

The 3rd woe (v. 16-22): "Woe unto you, ye blind guides, which say, Whosoever shall swear by the temple, it is nothing; but whosoever shall swear by the gold of the temple, he is a debtor! Ye fools and blind: for whether is greater, the gold, or the temple that sanctifieth the gold? And Whosoever shall swear by the altar, it is nothing; but whosoever sweareth by the gift that is upon it, he is guilty. Ye fools and blind: for whether is greater, the gift, or the altar that sanctifieth the gift? Whoso therefore shall swear by the altar, sweareth by it, and by all things thereon. And whoso shall swear by the temple, sweareth by it, and by him that dwelleth therein. And he that shall swear by heaven, sweareth by the throne of God, and by him that sitteth thereon."

In the 3rd woe of Matthew 23, Jesus refers to the casuistic approach of oaths and vows that was enforced by the Pharisees. These rules, which included avoiding oaths made by holy things because they were as binding as making an oath directly to God, were efforts made by the Pharisees to make sure people correctly followed the law.

The 4th woe (v. 23-24):

"Woe unto you, scribes and Pharisees, hypocrites! for ye pay tithe of mint and anise and cummin, and have omitted the weightier matters of the law, judgment, mercy, and faith: these ought ye to have done, and not to leave the other undone. Ye blind guides, which strain at a gnat, and swallow a camel."

In this woe, Jesus is explaining how the teachers and Pharisees try to make themselves look good by tithing seasonings, which were above and beyond what the law required of them, but they neglected the things that matter such as treating people with justice, and mercy, and faithfulness. They tithed above what was required to look good. Verse 24 refers to straining out a gnat, a practice done to drinks to make them pure. Here Jesus is saying that the Pharisees worry about the small things but neglect the important (swallow a camel).

The 5th woe (v. 25-26): "Woe unto you, scribes and Pharisees, hypocrites! for ye make clean the outside of the cup and of the platter, but within they are full of extortion and excess. Thou blind Pharisee, cleanse first that which is within the cup and platter, that the outside of them may be clean also."

Here we see the simple case that even though the leaders appear righteous and clean on the outside, they are greedy and corrupt on the inside. Jesus tells them to first take care of the inside and the outside will follow.

The 6th woe (v. 27-28):

"Woe unto you, scribes and Pharisees, hypocrites! for ye are like unto whited sepulchres, which indeed appear beautiful outward, but are within full of dead men's bones, and of all uncleanness. Even so, ye also outwardly appear righteous unto men, but within ye are full of hypocrisy and iniquity."

In this 6th woe, Jesus is making the same point as that in the 5th. That is, the teachers' and Pharisees' outward appearance gives the impression that they are righteous people, but in their hearts they are wicked. At that time, tombs were whitewashed to make them more noticeable so that people could avoid their contact, as contact with the dead was considered impure.

The 7th woe (v. 29-32):

"Woe unto you, scribes and Pharisees, hypocrites! because ye build the tombs of the prophets and garnish the sepulchres of the righteous, And say, If we had been in the days of our fathers, we would not have been partakers with them in the blood of the prophets. Wherefore ye be witnesses unto yourselves, that ye are the children of them which killed the prophets. Fill ye up then the measure of your fathers."

In this 7th and final woe, Jesus refers to Israel's rejection of prophets that God had sent them, and tradition had said that these prophets had been murdered. The Pharisees tried to atone for their fathers' sins by building monuments to commemorate the prophets and they claimed that they would have not participated in the killing of prophets as their fathers did. It seems that Jesus, though, is telling them that they are in reality just like their fathers.

The Lament of Jerusalem (v. 33-39):

> "Ye serpents, ye generation of vipers, how can ye escape the damnation of hell? Wherefore, behold, I send unto you prophets, and wise men, and scribes: and some of them ye shall kill and crucify; and some of them shall ye scourge in your synagogues, and persecute them from city to city: That upon you may come all the righteous blood shed upon the earth, from the blood of righteous Abel unto the blood of Zacharias son of Barachias, whom ye slew between the temple and the altar. Verily I say unto you, All these things shall come upon this generation. O Jerusalem, Jerusalem, thou that killest the prophets, and stonest them which are sent unto thee, how often would I have gathered thy children together, even as a hen gathereth her chickens under her wings, and ye would not! Behold, your house is left unto you desolate. For I say unto you, Ye shall not see me henceforth, till ye shall say, Blessed is he that cometh in the name of the Lord."

At the end of this chapter, Jesus laments Jerusalem and her people. He says that he is sending them prophets, wise men, and teachers, which many believe refer to Himself and His disciples that bring the message of Jesus. These men will undoubtedly be persecuted by many, and the Gospel will be rejected by the people, just as the Pharisees have rejected it. Because the Israelites will reject Jesus and His teachings, their "house" (believed to be the Temple), will be left desolate. To conclude this chapter, Jesus says, "You will not see me again until you say, 'Blessed is he who comes in the name of the Lord." This is most likely referring to Jesus' second coming, when the people who have rejected Jesus will say this, not in joy but in distress, for they know they will have to face judgment.

The Pharisees were people from a religious group called Chasidim, which was brought about after the resettling of Jewish people in Judea after the Babylonian captivity. The Chasidim followed the Law of Moses, as well as added traditions and observances to be followed. The Pharisees thought of themselves as holier than the common people.

As a Christian, you should avoid the pride and self-righteousness of the Pharisees which Jesus condemned in Matthew 23 and other Scriptural passages. Do not view yourself as better and deserving of praise from other people. Be careful not to boast and do not believe that you are better than the non-believers.

If you receive the grace to be in a leadership position within and outside the church, do not act like you are on a pedestal and behave very selfishly. Remember, "whoever exalts himself will be humbled, and whoever humbles himself will be exalted." Be humble and follow the example of Jesus Christ.

OTHER BIBLE PASSAGES ON THE SELF-RIGHTEOUSNESS OF THE PHARISEES

We found the Pharisees self-righteously judging others on the following passages of the Bible:

> Mark 14:4-10 – "Why was this waste ... made? For it might have been sold... they murmured? Judas ... went to betray him."

> Luke 15:2 – "The Pharisees murmured, This man receiveth sinners."

Luke 19:7 – "When (the Pharisees) saw it, they all murmured … he has gone to be a guest with … a sinner."

Matthew 9:10-13 – "And as Jesus passed forth from thence, he saw a man, named Matthew, sitting at the receipt of custom: and he saith unto him, Follow me. And he arose and followed him. And it came to pass, as Jesus sat at meat in the house, behold, many publicans and sinners came and sat down with him and his disciples. And when the Pharisees saw it, they said unto his disciples, Why eateth your Master with publicans and sinners? "But when Jesus heard that, he said unto them, They that be whole need not a physician, but they that are sick. But go ye and learn what that meaneth, I will have mercy and not sacrifice: for I am not come to call the righteous, but sinners to repentance." Jesus' response revealed the error in the thinking and conduct of the Pharisees."

THE LAODECIAN CHURCH

This is one of the seven churches in Asia Minor that Jesus sent His angel to address. The Laodecian church is guilty of self-righteousness, arising from the attitude of self-sufficiency and this also led to spiritual apathy on the part of the church.

Revelation 3:14-17

"And unto the angel of the church of the Laodecians write; These things saith the Amen, the faithful and true witness, the beginning of the creation of God. I know thy works, that thou art neither cold nor hot: I would thou wert cold or hot. So then because thou art lukewarm, and neither cold nor hot, I will spue thee out of my mouth. Because thou sayest, I am rich, and increased with goods, and have need of nothing; and knowest not that thou art wretched, and miserable, and poor, and blind, and naked."

The Laodecian church's self-righteous and self-sufficient attitude is seen in the Lord's diagnosis of its ills, "Because thou sayest, I am rich and increased with goods, and have need of nothing, and knowest not that thou art wretched, and miserable, and poor, and blind, and naked." One of the major undoings of the self-righteous person or church is that they put up the attitude of "I have it all and know it all. I don't need anyone or anything." In reality, they are wrong because they are in lack, blind, and grossly in need of help! Whether as an individual believer or a church, the Lord wants us to learn from the Laodecian church and not fall into its pit of error. Self-righteousness is counter-productive and sinful.

BALAAM'S SELF-RIGHTEOUSNESS

In Numbers 22, 23, and 24, the Bible records the story of Balaam from whom Balak, the king of Midian sought help to curse Israel because he feared that Israel would defeat and destroy them as it did to the Amorites. King Balak sent the elders of Midian to Balaam with precious rewards of divination. When the elders of Midian got to Balaam and delivered the message of their king, God came to Balaam and instructed him not to go with the elders of Midian and not to curse Israel because He had blessed them. Balaam told the elders of Midian that God had refused him to go with them. So, the elders departed disappointed.

However, King Balak did not give up. He sent again princes, more honorable than the first batch of emissaries.

Numbers 22:15-21

"And Balak sent yet again princes, more, and more honourable than they. And they came to Balaam, and said to him, Thus saith Balak the son of Zippor, Let nothing, I pray thee, hinder thee from coming unto me: For I will promote thee unto very great honour, and I will do whatsoever thou sayest unto me: come therefore, I pray thee, curse me this people. And Balaam answered and said unto the servants of Balak, If Balak would give me his house full of silver and gold, I cannot go beyond the word of the Lord my God, to do less or more. Now therefore, I pray you, tarry ye also here this night, that I may know what the Lord will say unto me more. And God came unto Balaam at night, and said unto him If the men come to call thee, rise up, and go with them; but yet the word which I shall say unto thee, that shalt thou do. And Balaam rose up in the morning, and saddled his ass, and went with the princes of Moab."

Balak craftily managed the temptation. The messengers he sent were more, and more honorable. He sent to Balaam (the conjurer) with as great respect and deference to his quality as if he had been a sovereign prince, thinking perhaps that Balaam had thought himself slighted in the fewness and meanness of the former messengers. The request was very urgent. This powerful prince becomes a suitor to him: "Let nothing, I pray thee, hinder thee (v. 16), no, not God, nor conscience, nor any fear either of sin or shame." Balak also made very attractive offers to Balaam: "I will promote thee to very great honor among the princes of Moab." He also gave Balaam a blank cheque to write his own terms: "I will do whatsoever thou sayest." That is, "I will give you whatever you desire, and do whatever you order; your word shall be a law to me. He was ready and willing to do anything for Balaam to just curse Israel.

Balaam's self-righteousness lies in his knowing God's position in this matter: (1) "Don't go with them. (2) Don't curse Israel because I have blessed them." Then while Balaam appears to be resistant to the demand and pressure of King Balak, he was really yielding to the temptation. God sees the heart and nothing is hidden from Him. There is an apparent struggle in Balaam between his convictions and his corruption. His convictions made him to say, "If Balak would give me his house full of silver and gold, and that is more than he can give or I can ask, I cannot go beyond the word of the Lord my God." Here, he honored God with his mouth. Did his heart honor God as well?

Having received the clear commandment of God not to go with the Midianites and not to curse Israel as Balak had demanded.

Balaam should not have told the Midianite emissaries to tarry for the night for him to inquire of the matter from the Lord a second time. He did this because his heart was not right with God. His covetousness and corruption got the better part of him. He was not promptly, unquestioningly, and completely obedient to God. It was out of annoyance and permissive will that God told him in Numbers 22:19 to go with the Midianite emissaries. God again added that even if Balaam goes with them, he should do only what He asks him to do. In Numbers 22:22, the Bible says that God's anger was kindled because Balaam went with the Midianite emissaries to see Balak.

Balaam's self-righteous attitude is despicable, and God was not happy about it. He went on to build altars, engage in divination and sought to please Balak rather than God. He was heavily blinded by covetousness and the love of material gain and fame. He relied heavily on his gifts and the gains they attracted rather than on God. He sought his own glory rather than God's glory. Balaam is an example of professed Christians today who claim to operate in the gifts of the Holy Spirit, but their hearts are not right with God, and they only seek to satisfy their bellies and egos, rather than seek to build God's kingdom and give all the glory to Him. Balaam spoke honourably of Jehovah with his mouth, but he did not obey His express and clear instructions. Beloved, beware of Balaam's trap and self-righteous attitude!

PETER'S SELF-RIGHTEOUSNESS

Galatians 2:11-21

"But when Peter was come to Antioch, I withstood him to the face, because he was to be blamed. For before that certain came from James, he did eat with the Gentiles: but when they were come, he withdrew and separated himself, fearing them which were of the circumcision. And the other Jews dissembled likewise with him; insomuch that Barnabas also was carried away with their dissimulation. But when I saw that they walked not uprightly according to the truth of the gospel, I said unto Peter before them all, If thou, being a Jew, livest after the manner of Gentiles, and not as do the Jews, why compellest thou the Gentiles to live as do the Jews? We who are Jews by nature, and not sinners of the Gentiles, Knowing that a man is not justified by the works of the law, but by the faith of Jesus Christ, even we have believed in Jesus Christ, that we might be justified by the faith of Christ, and not by the works of the law: for by the works of the law shall no flesh be justified. But if, while we seek to be justified by Christ, we ourselves also are found sinners, is therefore Christ the minister of sin? God forbid. For if I build again the things which I destroyed, I make myself a transgressor. For I through the law am dead to the law, that I might live unto God. I am crucified with Christ: nevertheless I live; yet not I, but Christ liveth in me: and the life which I now live in the flesh I live by the faith of the Son of God, who loved me and gave himself for me. I do not frustrate the grace of God: for if righteousness come by the law, then Christ is dead in vain."

The important lesson here is that believers who think they stand should be careful so that they do not fall. Apostle Peter was a foremost apostle. Yet he fell into the error of self-righteousness. Apostle Paul had to bravely point out Peter's mistake to him and others, correcting the self-righteous attitude.

Paul spoke against self-righteousness. He adhered resolutely to his principles when others faltered in theirs; he was as good a Jew as any of them (for he was a Hebrew of the Hebrews), but he would magnify his office as the apostle of the Gentiles, and therefore would not see them discouraged and trampled upon. When he saw that some apostles walked not uprightly, according to the truth of the gospel—that they did not live up to that principle which the gospel taught, and which they had professed to own and embrace, namely, that by the death of Christ the partition-wall between Jew and Gentile was taken down, and the observance of the law of Moses was no longer in force—when he observed this, as Peter's offense was public, so he publicly reproved him for it. He said unto Peter before them all, "If thou, being a Jew, livest after the manner of the Gentiles, and not as do the Jews, why compellest thou the Gentiles to live as do the Jews?" Herein one part of Peter's conduct was a contradiction to the other; for if he, who was a Jew, could himself sometimes dispense with the use of the ceremonial law, and live after the manner of the Gentiles, this showed that he did not look upon the observance of it as still necessary, even for the Jews themselves; and therefore that he could not, consistently with his practice, impose it upon the Gentile Christians. And yet Paul charges him with this, yea, represents him as compelling the Gentiles to live as did the Jews—not by open force and violence, but this was the tendency of what he did; for it was in effect to signify this, that the Gentiles must comply with the Jews, or else not be admitted into Christian communion. This was a self-righteous attitude on the part of Peter. It needed to be corrected and Paul did so.

By so doing, Paul also established that great fundamental doctrine of the gospel—That justification is only by faith in Christ, and not by the works of the law (though some think that all he says to the end of the chapter is what he said to Peter at Antioch), which doctrine condemned Peter for his symbolizing with the Jews. For, if it was the principle of his religion that the gospel is the instrument of our justification and not the law, then he did very ill in countenancing those who kept up the law and were for mixing it with faith in the business of our justification. This was the doctrine that Paul had preached among the Galatians, to which he still adhered, and which it is his great business in this epistle to mention and comment.

FOUR

MANIFESTATIONS OF SELF-RIGHTEOUSNESS

I know it is of great importance that all believers know what constitutes self-righteousness and how it manifests in the lives of individuals and the body of Christ. This will help us to prevent it and to cure it if we ever get into its trap. Here are some of the manifestations of self-righteousness as revealed by the Bible.

1. **The self-righteous refuse Jesus' salvation:** In what way do they do this? First, they deny the centrality and indispensability of grace and rely on works. Second, they deny the truth about the atoning and substitutionary work of Jesus Christ as the source of our justification (forgiveness and righteousness) and see the law as all in all. Third, they see no need for the Saviour and believe erroneously that they do not need salvation because they claim to be healthy, complete, and self-sufficient. The following Scriptures lend credence to this truth:

Matthew 5:20

"For I say unto you, That except your righteousness shall exceed the righteousness of the scribes and Pharisees, ye shall in no case enter into the kingdom of heaven."

Matthew 9:10-13

While Jesus was having dinner at Matthew's house, many tax collectors and "sinners" came and ate with him and his disciples. When the Pharisees saw this, they asked his disciples, "Why does your teacher eat with tax collectors and 'sinners'?" On hearing this, Jesus said, "It is not the healthy who need a doctor, but the sick. But go and learn what this means: 'I desire mercy, not sacrifice.' For I have not come to call the righteous, but sinners."

Matthew 9: 21-31

"For she said within herself, If I may but touch his garment, I shall be whole. But Jesus turned him about, and when he saw her, he said, Daughter, be of good comfort; thy faith hath made thee whole. And the woman was made whole from that hour. And when Jesus came into the ruler's house and saw the minstrels and the people making a noise, He said unto them, Give place: for the maid is not dead, but sleepeth. And they laughed him to scorn. But when the people were put forth, he went in, and took her by the hand, and the maid arose. And the fame hereof went abroad into all that land. And when Jesus departed thence, two blind men followed him, crying, and saying, Thou Son of David, have mercy on us. And when he was come into the house, the blind men came to him: and Jesus saith unto them, Believe ye that I am able to do this? They said unto him, Yea, Lord. Then touched he their eyes, saying, According to your faith be it unto you. And their eyes were opened; and Jesus straitly charged them, saying, See that no man know it. But they, when they were departed, spread abroad his fame in all that country."

John 5:39-45

"Search the scriptures; for in them ye think ye have eternal life: and they are they which testify of me. And ye will not come to me, that ye might have life. I receive not honour from men. But I know you, that ye have not the love of God in you. I am come in my Father's name, and ye receive me not: if another shall come in his own name, him ye will receive. How can ye believe, which receive honour one of another, and seek not the honour that cometh from God only?"

Romans 10:3-4

"For they being ignorant of God's righteousness, and going about to establish their own righteousness, have not submitted themselves unto the righteousness of God. For Christ is the end of the law for righteousness to everyone that believeth."

1 John 1:9-10

"If we confess our sins, he is faithful and just to forgive us our sins, and to cleanse us from all unrighteousness. If we say that we have not sinned, we make him a liar, and his word is not in us."

2. **Self-righteousness manifests in legalism and denies Jesus' sacrifice:** The truth of the gospel is that no one can be truly righteous without believing and accepting the sacrifice of Jesus Christ, the Son of God, as the only route to salvation and justification. Yet, this is the greatest manifestation of self-righteousness. Some religious adherents do not believe that Jesus died on the Cross as the ultimate sacrifice and redemption for mankind. They seek salvation through their works. What a pity!

   Romans 10:3 says, "Going about to establish their own righteousness have not submitted themselves unto the righteousness of God."

   Galatians 2:21 affirms, "If righteousness comes by the law, then Christ is dead in vain (no reason)." The Law can't save anyone or make anyone righteous. That is why Acts 13:39 adds, "By him all that believe are justified from all things, from which ye could not be justified by the Law." Israel, which followed after the law of righteousness, hath not attained to the law of righteousness (Romans 9:31-32). Apostle Paul explained that he did not have his own righteousness, which is of the law, but that which is through the faith of Christ (Philippians 3:3-9). I encourage you to imitate him.

3. **The Self-Righteous act hypocritically:** This attitude manifests in different ways. The self-righteous person is proud, loves to pray publicly, seeks attention and praise for self rather than God, sees himself or herself as being better than or superior to others, and loves to pray long, repetitive prayers (Matthew 6:5-6, Luke 18:10-14, Matthew 6:7-8, Matthew 23:14).

4. **The Self-righteous judges others and do not show mercy:** The Lord commands us to forgive those who hurt us or despitefully use us. God spoke woe to the unmerciful. Matthew 6:15 says, "If ye forgive not men their trespasses, neither will (God) forgive your trespasses." Matthew 18:23-35 adds, "So … shall (God) do also unto you, of ye … forgive not everyone his brother and their trespasses." God commands us to forgive others and show them mercy so that we too can enjoy His mercy. James 2:13 underscores this truth, "He shall have judgment without mercy, that hath showed no mercy." The self-righteous feel they do not sin and do not need forgiveness; therefore they are unloving and unforgiving to others:

Luke 7:47 says, "To whom little is forgiven, the same loveth little." In Luke 15:25-30, the Bible reveals that the faithful older brother was angry that his father forgave the penitent Prodigal Son. Luke 18:9 also says that certain trusted in themselves that they were righteous, and (therefore) despised others.

Other manifestations of the self-righteously judging others include:

Mark 14:4-10 – "Why was this waste …made? For it might have been sold… they murmured? Judas … went to betray him." Luke 15:2 – "The Pharisees murmured, This man receiveth sinners." Luke 19:7 – "When (the Pharisees) saw it, they all murmured … he has gone to be a guest with … a sinner."

5. **Self-righteous manifests in misguided religious zeal:** Those who are gripped by the spirit of religious zeal always think that they are doing service to God and His kingdom when in reality they are doing a disservice to heaven. Also, in John 16:2, the Bible says that whosoever killeth you will think that he doeth God service. In Acts 13:50, the hypocritical and self-righteous Jews stirred up the devout and honorable women.

Similarly, Apostle Paul, before his conversion, manifested a self-righteous attitude by attacking Christians, killing, and persecuting the early church. He had misguided religious zeal. In Acts 22:3-4, he confessed, "Zealous … I persecuted this way unto the death."

The following statements are also attributed to Paul: Acts 26:9-11, "I thought I ought to do many things contrary to Jesus." Galatians 1: 13-14, "Persecuted ... being exceedingly zealous of traditions" and Philippians 3:6, "Concerning zeal, persecuting the church." Thank God for the encounter that Paul had with Jesus and the supernatural transformation the Lord gave his life and destiny.

Another account in the Bible that reveals the manifestation of self-righteousness is in Acts 23:12:14, - 40 men vowed and conspired to kill Paul. They bound themselves with an oath and fasted, saying they would not stop until they had killed Paul. These people were victims of self-righteousness fuelled by religious zeal.

6. **Self-righteousness borders on hypocrisy:** Some people appear outwardly good but are inwardly wicked. Matthew 7:15 says that they are in sheep's clothing, but inwardly they are ravening wolves. Matthew 23:5 says, "that all their works they do for to be seen of men." Matthew 23:27-28 adds that "like unto whited sepulchres, which indeed appear beautiful outward ... full of hypocrisy and iniquity." Luke 18:11-12 reveals the pride and self-righteous attitude of the Pharisee, "I thank thee, that I am not as ... this publican. I fast."

7. **Self-righteousness manifests in false holiness and religious standards:** This is best found in the lives of the Pharisees and Jesus condemned their acts heavily. In Matthew 23:4, Jesus said that the self-righteous bind heavy burdens ... on men's shoulders. Acts 15:10 reveals that one of the manifestations of self-righteousness includes putting a yoke upon the neck of the disciples. **The Bible warns believers to steer clear of self-righteous attitudes at all times.**

FIVE

THE DANGERS OF
SELF-RIGHTEOUSNESS

Self-righteousness is unbiblical, ungodly, and not Christlike. In the preceding chapters, we saw that both Christians and non-Christians demonstrate self-righteous attitudes. In the Old Testament, Job was self-righteous but he repented when his mistake was brought to his notice. Balaam was self-righteous too. In the New Testament, the Pharisees were self-righteously hypocritical and Jesus condemned it. Peter was self-righteous on an occasion and Paul corrected him. The spirit of self-righteousness can also be found in a church as we saw in the Laodecian church (Revelation 3).

The victims of self-righteousness are guilty because they violate a major or cardinal biblical principle and kingdom ordinance that forgiveness, righteousness, justification, and salvation cannot be obtained through the law or works but by the grace of God that is only imputed to us through the finished work of Jesus Christ and by faith. Self-righteousness can send its victim to hell. Therefore, in this chapter, we shall focus on the dangers of self-righteousness.

1. **SELF-RIGHTEOUSNESS MAKES US THINK THAT WE – IN OURSELVES – ARE GOOD AND RIGHTEOUS**

Self-righteousness makes us think we are good and righteous in ourselves. We are not and this must be corrected otherwise we face disastrous consequences. In Job 15:14-16, the Bible says, "What is man, that he should be clean? ... righteous?... the heavens are not clean in His sight. How much more abominable and filthy is man." The truth is that we can only be truly clean, pure, good, and righteous if God makes us so. We cannot achieve this status on our own. We need God's grace and faith in His works of redemption to have them.

The Bible says that all have sinned and fallen short of the glory of God. Romans 3:23-24, "for all have sinned and fall short of the glory of God, and all are justified freely by his grace through the redemption that came by Christ Jesus." That sin and its consequences can only be removed or remitted by the blood of Jesus. Psalm 10:3 confirms man's sinful and hopeless state before salvation, "If thou shouldest mark iniquities, who shall stand?" Similarly, Proverbs 20:9 asks, "Who can say, I have made my heart clean, I am pure?" The Bible provides these answers: Ecclesiastes 7:20 – There is not a just man upon earth, that doeth good and sinneth not. Isaiah 64:6 adds, "We are all as an unclean thing, and all our righteousness is as filthy rags." Romans 3:10, 23 – "There is none righteous, no, not one ... all have sinned" and Romans 7: 18 – "In me, that is, in my flesh, dwelleth no good thing."

Secondly, we are not good and righteous in ourselves because only God is good. The Scriptures affirm this truth in Job 9:2, "But how should man be just with God?" Psalm 71: 16 says, "I will make mention of thy righteousness, thine only." Matthew 19: 17 adds, "There is none good but one, that is, God."

Thirdly, being self-righteous by saying that we are good and righteous all by ourselves causes us to be lifted up in pride. Proverbs 30: 12-13 says, "They are pure in their own eyes ... O how lofty are their eyes! And their eyelids are lifted up." We saw pride in the hypocritical and self-righteous Pharisee's prayer in Luke 18:11. He said, "God, I thank thee, that I am not as other men... unjust." Of course, the Pharisees did not go home justified. The reason is that God gives grace to the humble and exalts him while he abases the proud. This is one danger of self-righteousness we cannot afford to ignore!

2. SELF-RIGHTEOUSNESS SEPARATES US FROM GOD

The implication of self-righteousness is that the victims are guilty of going about to establish their own righteousness and have not submitted unto the righteousness of God (Romans 10:3). This a grievous sin in the sight of God and it separates the sinner from His Maker. Job was guilty of it and had to repent for him to enjoy the best God had for him. This is what every believer who is guilty of self-righteousness must do. In Job 13:16, the Bible says, "A hypocrite shall not come before him." A self-righteous person is a hypocrite in God's estimation.

3. SELF-RIGHTEOUSNESS MAKES US UNABLE TO SEE OUR SINS

One of the dangers of self-righteousness is that it promotes self-deceit and pride. The victim develops and exhibits the attitude of self-sufficiency and is unable to see his or her sins and faults. Job 32:1 says that Job was righteous in his own eyes. Proverbs 16:2 and 21:2 say, "that all the ways of a man are clean in his own eyes but the LORD ponders the hearts and weighs the spirits."

Today, we have a generation that is pure in their own eyes, and yet is not washed from their filthiness (Proverbs 30:12). This is another consequence of self-righteousness. They are unclean, yet they think they are clean. As a result, they reject or miss the grace or opportunity to be cleansed. This is the same way the rich young ruler missed the offer of eternal life that Jesus gave him! It is also the same way the Pharisees had encounters with Jesus, heard His rebuke on self-righteousness but did not repent and avail themselves of the divine opportunities. Luke 6:41-42 affirms the pitiable state of the self-righteous individual. "And why do you look at the speck in your brother's eye, but do not perceive the plank in your own eye? Or how can you say to your brother, 'Brother, let me **remove the speck that *is* in your eye,' when you yourself do not** see the plank that *is* in your own eye? Hypocrite! First remove the plank from your own eye, and then you will see clearly to remove the speck that is in your brother's eye."

4. SELF-RIGHTEOUNESS IS THE ABSENCE OF TRUE RIGHTEOUNSNESS

True righteousness means trusting God and not laying claim to any righteousness of one's own or relying on one's work. Abraham and Paul were shining examples of believers who demonstrated true righteousness in the Bible. Galatians 3:6 says that Abraham believed God, it was accounted righteousness. Philippians 3:9 also says about Paul, "Not having mine own righteousness... but ... of God." Do you have your own righteousness? Examine yourself. Only the righteousness that God gives to His own can give justification.

Self-righteousness, on the other hand, attracts divine wrath and judgment. That is why the Bible clearly affirms in Titus 3:5, "Not by works of righteousness which we have done, but according to his mercy he saved us." The evil of self-righteousness is that the victim operates outside the mercy and grace of God. Such victims end up as spiritual failures and losers. True believers would always go boldly to the throne of grace to receive mercy, grace, and help in a time of need. (Hebrews 4:14). They depend on God's grace, mercy, and help, not on their own works or ability. They always declare that their sufficiency is of God.

5. SELF-RIGHTEOUSNESS MAKES YOU THINK THAT YOU – IN YOURSELF – ARE BETTER THAN OTHERS

The truth of the gospel is that you are not better than others. That is why the Bible admonishes us not to think too highly of ourselves but should always be humble and God will exalt us. In John 8, Jesus dealt with the problem of hypocritical self-righteous attitude in the lives of the scribes and Pharisees who caught a woman in the very act of adultery and were bent on judging her severely. They insisted that the law of Moses commanded that such an offender should be stoned and sought Jesus' view. In John 8:7, Jesus told the tempters (the scribes and the Pharisees, "He that is without sin... let him first cast a stone." The Bible affirms that, when they heard this, they were convicted by their own conscience, and they went one by one, leaving the woman untouched. Jesus lifted up Himself and asked, "Woman, where are your accusers? Has no man condemned you?" The woman answered, "No man, Lord." Jesus replied, "Neither do I condemn you. Go and sin no more."

Self-righteousness makes people forget that all have sinned and come short of the glory of God (Romans 3:23). It also makes people judgmental rather than show mercy as God has commanded.

6. SELF-RIGHTEOUNESS PRODUCES A PROUD ATTITUDE THAT DISPLEASES AND ANGERS GOD

God judges pride because He will never share His glory with anyone. Pride births and promotes self. The victim of pride and self-righteousness always draw attention to themselves, seek to please themselves, win attention to themselves, and seek their own gains and glory rather than God's. They also attribute their achievements to their personal efforts, abilities, and wisdom rather than attributing them to God, the source from which all good things and blessings flow. Prophet Isaiah declares that they say, "I am holier than thou." These are as smoke in my (God's) nose. Similarly, in Luke 16:15, Jesus said of the self-righteous, "Ye are they which justify yourselves ... but ... that which is highly esteemed among men is an abomination (to) God."

7. SELF-RIGHTEOUSNESS MAKES US DESPISE AND BE UNMERCIFUL TO OTHERS

The sin of the Pharisee in the popular story of the two that went to pray in the temple is that of despising others. In Luke 18:11, the Pharisee said, "God, I thank thee, that I am not as other men are... unjust or even as this publican (tax collector)." He was praying amiss. God does not want us to despise other people or act as if we are better than them. We are to love one another and honor others always. Luke 18:9 says, "They trusted in themselves that they were righteous, and despised others." We should avoid this.

The Bible also condemns the Pharisees in Matthew 23:23 for paying tithes but omits the weightier and more important matters of the law like mercy. Jesus added that they should have concentrated on carrying out the acts of mercy consistently but have left that undone. Heaven will richly reward you for weightier matters such as mercy, faith, and judgment.

SIX

BIBLICAL VERSES OF SELF-RIGHTEOUSNESS

The word of God is perfect converting the soul and making wise the simple (Psalm 19:7). It is in God's word that the believer can find timeless truths and guidance on any subject as well as solutions to major issues of life. God's word is inerrant, immutable, and the cure to all human ills. The following passages of the Bible provide insights and illumination into the subject of self-righteousness. As you read and apply them, you will live in righteousness and enjoy its fruits. You will not be a victim of self-righteousness, in the name of Jesus.

1 Corinthians 4:7 – "For who maketh thee to differ from another? and what hast thou that thou didst not receive? now if thou didst receive it, why dost thou glory, as if thou hadst not received it?"

1 John 1:9 – "If we confess our sins, he is faithful and just to forgive us our sins, and to cleanse us from all unrighteousness."

1 Timothy 5:8 – "But if any provide not for his own, and specially for those of his own house, he hath denied the faith, and is worse than an infidel."

2 Cor. 5:21 - "For he hath made him to be sin for us, who knew no sin; that we might be made the righteousness of God in him."

2 Pet. 3:9 – "The Lord is not slack concerning his promise, as some men count slackness; but is longsuffering to us-ward, not willing that any should perish, but that all should come to repentance."

2 Timothy 1:7- "For God hath not given us the spirit of fear; but of power, and of love, and of a sound mind."

Ezekiel 18:20 – "The soul that sinneth, it shall die. The son shall not bear the iniquity of the father, neither shall the father bear the iniquity of the son: the righteousness of the righteous shall be upon him, and the wickedness of the wicked shall be upon him."

Galatians 2:16 – "Knowing that a man is not justified by the works of the law, but by the faith of Jesus Christ, even we have believed in Jesus Christ, that we might be justified by the faith of Christ, and not by the works of the law: for by the works of the law shall no flesh be justified."

Isaiah 46:12 – "Hearken unto me, ye stout-hearted, that are far from righteousness."

Isaiah 64:6 – "But we are all as an unclean thing, and all our righteousness are as filthy rags; and we all do fade as a leaf; and our iniquities, like the wind, have taken us away."

Isaiah 65:5 – "Which say, Stand by thyself, come not near to me; for I am holier than thou. These are a smoke in my nose, a fire that burneth all the day."

James 3:18 – "And the fruit of righteousness is sown in peace of them that make peace."

John 14:15 – "If ye love me, keep my commandments."

Luke 10:27 – "And he answering said, Thou shalt love the Lord thy God with all thy heart, and with all thy soul, and with all thy strength, and with all thy mind; and thy neighbor as thyself."

Mark 12:30 – "And thou shalt love the Lord thy God with all thy heart, and with all thy soul, and with all thy mind, and with all thy strength: this is the first commandment."

Mark 12:31 – "And the second is like, namely this, Thou shalt love thy neighbour as thyself. There is none other commandment greater than these."

Matthew 6:7 – "But when ye pray, use not vain repetitions, as the heathen do: for they think that they shall be heard for their much speaking."

Proverbs 30:12 – "There is a generation that are pure in their own eyes, and yet is not washed from their filthiness."

Psalm 12:4 – "Who have said, With our tongue will we prevail; our lips are our own: who is lord over us?"

Romans 10:3 – "For they being ignorant of God's righteousness, and going about to establish their own righteousness, have not submitted themselves unto the righteousness of God."

Romans 12: 19 – "Dearly beloved, avenge not yourselves, but rather give place unto wrath: for it is written, Vengeance is mine; I will repay, saith the Lord."

Rom. 14:1 – "Him that is weak in the faith receive ye, but not to doubtful disputations."

Rom. 8:7 – "Because the carnal mind is enmity against God: for it is not subject to the law of God, neither indeed can be."

Romans 10:3 – "For not knowing about God's righteousness and seeking to establish their own, they did not subject themselves to the righteousness of God."

Luke 10:29 – "But wishing to justify himself, he said to Jesus, "And who is my neighbors?"

Luke 18:9 – "And He also told this parable to some people who trusted in themselves that they were righteous, and viewed others with contempt."

Philippians 3:4-6 – "Although I myself might have confidence even in the flesh. If anyone else has a mind to put confidence in the flesh, I far more: circumcised the eighth day, of the nation of Israel, of the tribe of Benjamin, a Hebrew of Hebrews; as to the Law, a Pharisee; as to zeal, a persecutor of the church; as to the righteousness which is in the Law, found blameless."

1 John 1:8 – "If we say that we have no sin, we are deceiving ourselves and the truth is not in us."

Proverbs 20:9 – "Who can say, "I have cleansed my heart, I am pure from my sin?"

Hosea 12:8 – "And Ephraim said, "Surely I have become rich, I have found wealth for myself; In all my labors they will find in me. No iniquity, which would be sin."

Proverbs 16:2 – "All the ways of a man are clean in his own sight, But the Lord weighs the motives."

Jeremiah 2:34-35 - "Also on your skirts is found. The lifeblood of the innocent poor; You did not find them breaking in. But in spite of all these things, Yet you said, 'I am innocent; Surely His anger is turned away from me.' Behold, I will enter into judgment with you Because you say, 'I have not sinned."

Deuteronomy 9:4 - "Do not say in your heart when the Lord your God has driven them out before you, 'Because of my righteousness the Lord has brought me in to possess this land,' but it is because of the wickedness of these nations that the Lord is dispossessing them before you."

Ezekiel 28:2 - "Son of man, say to the leader of Tyre, 'Thus says the Lord God, Because your heart is lifted up. And you have said, 'I am a god, I sit in the seat of gods. In the heart of the seas'; Yet you are a man and not God, Although you make your heart like the heart of God."

1 John 1:5-6 – "This is the message we have heard from Him and announce to you, that God is Light, and in Him there is no darkness at all. If we say that we have fellowship with Him and yet walk in the darkness, we lie and do not practice the truth;"

Proverbs 30:12 – "There is a kind who is pure in his own eyes, Yet is not washed from his filthiness."

Jeremiah 17:9 – "The heart is more deceitful than all else. And is desperately sick; Who can understand it?"

Matthew 23:23-2 - "Woe to you, scribes and Pharisees, hypocrites! For you tithe mint and dill and cummin, and have neglected the weightier provisions of the law: justice and mercy and faithfulness; but these are the things you should have done without neglecting the others. You blind guides, who strain out a gnat and swallow a camel!"

Luke 16:15 – "And He said to them, "You are those who justify yourselves in the sight of men, but God knows your hearts; for that which is highly esteemed among men is detestable in the sight of God."

Hebrews 3:13 – "But encourage one another day after day, as long as it is still called "Today," so that none of you will be hardened by the deceitfulness of sin."

Luke 18:9-11 – "And He also told this parable to some people who trusted in themselves that they were righteous, and viewed others with contempt: "Two men went up into the temple to pray, one a Pharisee and the other a tax collector. The Pharisee stood and was praying this to himself: 'God, I thank You that I am not like other people: swindlers, unjust, adulterers, or even like this tax collector."

Philippians 2:3 – "Do nothing from selfishness or empty conceit, but with humility of mind regard one another as more important than yourselves;"

Colossians 2:16-18 – "Therefore no one is to act as your judge in regard to food or drink or in respect to a festival or a new moon or a Sabbath day— things which are a mere shadow of what is to come; but the substance belongs to Christ. Let no one keep defrauding you of your prize by delighting in self-abasement and the worship of the angels, taking his stand on visions he has seen, inflated without cause by his fleshly mind."

1 John 1:10 – "If we say that we have not sinned, we make Him a liar and His word is not in us."

Zephaniah 3:11 - "In that day you will feel no shame because of all your deeds by which you have rebelled against Me; For then I will remove from your midst Your proud, exulting ones, And you will never again be haughty on My holy mountain."

2 Corinthians 10:18 – "For it is not he who commends himself that is approved, but he whom the Lord commends."

Galatians 5:4 – "You have been severed from Christ, you who are seeking to be justified by law; you have fallen from grace."

Numbers 16: - "They assembled together against Moses and Aaron, and said to them, "You have gone far enough, for all the congregation are holy, every one of them, and the Lord is in their midst; so why do you exalt yourselves above the assembly of the Lord?"

1 Samuel 15:13-21 – "Samuel came to Saul, and Saul said to him, "Blessed are you of the Lord! I have carried out the command of the Lord." But Samuel said, "What then is this bleating of the sheep in my ears and the lowing of the oxen which I hear?" Saul said, "They have brought them from the Amalekites, for the people spared the best of the sheep and oxen, to sacrifice to the Lord your God; but the rest we have utterly destroyed."

Psalm 10:5 – "His ways prosper at all times; Your judgments are on high, out of his sight; As for all his adversaries, he snorts at them."

Luke 16:14 – "Now the Pharisees, who were lovers of money, were listening to all these things and were scoffing at Him."

Luke 18:9-14 – "And He also told this parable to some people who trusted in themselves that they were righteous, and viewed others with contempt: "Two men went up into the temple to pray, one a Pharisee and the other a tax collector. The Pharisee stood and was praying this to himself: 'God, I thank You that I am not like other people: swindlers, unjust, adulterers, or even like this tax collector."

John 9:39-41 – "And Jesus said, "For judgment, I came into this world, so that those who do not see may see, and that those who see may become blind." Those of the Pharisees who were with Him heard these things and said to Him, "We are not blind too, are we?" Jesus said to them, "If you were blind, you would have no sin; but since you say, 'We see,' your sin remains."

Revelation 3:17-18 "Because you say, "I am rich, and have become wealthy, and have need of nothing," and you do not know that you are wretched and miserable and poor and blind and naked, I advise you to buy from Me gold refined by fire so that you may become rich, and white garments so that you may clothe yourself, and that the shame of your nakedness will not be revealed; and eye salve to anoint your eyes so that you may see."

SEVEN

HOW TO BE FREE FROM
SELF-RIGHTEOUSNESS

The good news for all believers is that God did not only despise and punish self-righteousness. He is gracious enough to provide cures for it. What are the ways out of the problem of self-righteousness in the Bible? This chapter shall treat some of these so that we avoid the trap and those who have fallen into it might get saved.

1. WE ONLY ARE WHAT WE ARE BY GOD'S GRACE

The timeless truth that all believers need to know and always remember is that we are only what we are by the grace of God. This was Paul's declaration and it is quite apt. If we always bear this in mind, we will not become proud, hypocritical, judgmental, unmerciful, quick to condemn, despise others and demonstrate a self-sufficient attitude. Like Paul, let us always confess: By the grace of God I am what I am (1 Corinthians 15:10).

The Bible asks this very important question: "Who maketh thee to differ from another? And what hast thou that thou didst not receive?" (1 Corinthians 4:7). Paul, the distinguished apostle who deserves our emulation, said this in 2 Corinthians 3:5, "Not that we are sufficient of ourselves to think anything as of ourselves." These are the cures and antidotes to self-righteousness. Let us take a cue from the Bible and the distinguished Apostle Paul!

2. BLESSED ARE THE POOR IN SPIRIT

In Matthew 5:3, the Bible says, "Blessed are the poor in spirit for there is the kingdom of heaven." Self-righteousness is a spirit; it is also an attitude. What opens the doorway for this spirit is pride. So, when you are poor in spirit, you are humble, and lowly in your own eyes. You are teachable and obedient to the Lord. The poor in spirit are also self-denying, at ease, like little children in your own opinion they are considered to be weak, foolish, and insignificant.

It is to look with a holy contempt upon ourselves self-righteousness, to value others, and not to compare ourselves to them. It is to be willing to make ourselves do good; to become all things to all men. It is to acknowledge that God is greater than the greatest and that all good things come from God. It is to affirm that He is Holy and we are redeemed; that He is all and without Him we can do nothing good that has eternal value. We must trust, obey, and humble ourselves before God, and walk safely under His mighty hand.

It is to come off from all confidence in our righteousness and strength, that we may depend only upon the merit of Christ for our justification and the spirit and grace of Christ for our sanctification. That broken and contrite spirit with which the publican cried for mercy to a poor sinner, is that poverty of spirit. We must call ourselves poor in spirit, because always in want of God's grace. So "Let us, therefore, come boldly unto the throne of grace, that we may obtain mercy, and find grace to help in time of need." Hebrews 4:16

The Bible adds that the kingdom of heaven belongs to those who are poor in spirit. They only are fit to be members of Christ's church, which is called the congregation of saints, the body of Christ (1 Corinthians 12:12-27); the kingdom of glory is prepared for them. Those who thus humble themselves, and comply with God when he humbles them, shall be thus exalted. The great, high spirits go away with the glory of the kingdoms of the earth; but the humble, mild, and yielding souls obtain the glory of the kingdom of heaven.

71

3. NOW THE TRUTH AND LET THE TRUTH SET YOU FREE

Ignorance of God's word and truth is a major cause of self-righteousness. The Bible says "And you shall know the truth and the truth shall set you free"- John 8:32. An important weapon to damage ignorance in our lives is to let the word of God dwell in us richly. The Bible affirms that "...... through knowledge the righteous shall be delivered" - Proverbs 11:9. Self-righteousness also thrives because of the preponderance of false teachings and false teachers today. The propagation of the enemy's lies and deceits has made many people reject the grace of God and His righteousness and seek their righteousness. The atoning sacrifice as well as the finished, complete, and perfect work of Jesus Christ on the cross earned us salvation, free. The atoning sacrifice is about the life and death of Christ, which brought about a restored relationship between God and mankind. For everyone who believe, the atoning work of Jesus Christ removed the barrier separating God and humanity. The self-righteous believes and says that the blood of Jesus is not price enough as atonement for our sins till man adds his work, silver, and gold. The implication of this is that Christ's blood is not our redemption at all and He is not our Redeemer.

Self-righteousness is teaching and holding that our Lord's bearing of sin for us did not make a perfect atonement and that it is ineffectual till we either do or suffer something to complete it, then in the supplemental work lies the real value, and Christ's work is in itself insufficient. If a believer in Christ is not completely saved by what Christ has done, but must do something himself to complete it, then salvation was not finished, and the Savior's work remains imperfect till mankind lends a hand to make up for His deficiencies.

The spirit of self-righteousness rejects the covenant which was sealed with Christ's death. If we can be saved by the old covenant of works, the new covenant was not required. The sacrifice of Jesus ratified the new covenant. No one was ever saved under the covenant of works nor ever will be, and the new covenant is introduced for that reason. The profound knowledge of this timeless truth is what is missing in many lives and this knowledge gap makes many people vulnerable to self-righteousness.

Therefore, the church must make the teaching of this truth about righteousness, justification, and salvation paramount. The more of this truth that people know, the more they will be free from the spirit and attitude of self-righteousness. God's word is a veritable weapon for overcoming self-righteousness.

4. PRAY SELF-RIGHTEOUSNESS OUT OF YOUR LIFE

Someone said, "Why worry when you can pray." This is the word of wisdom from Norman Vincent Peale in dealing with worry, "Say to yourself, why worry when you can pray?" The Psalmist says "I prayed to the Lord, and he answered me. He freed me from all my fears." Psalm 34:4. The ministry of the Word of God and prayer has brought innumerable blessings to the lives of individuals, churches, and organizations all over the world.

When the believer prays, Heaven's help is provided and things will change for good. You can pray against self-righteousness, anger, lust, failure, poverty, fear, anxiety, and anything detestable out of your life. The Bible says that "for this purpose, the son of God was manifested so that He might destroy the works of the devil." 1 John 3:8. Through prayer, the believer accesses the power and grace of Jesus Christ, the Son of God, and the impossible becomes possible. The Bible also affirms that "the effectual fervent prayer of the righteous avails much." James 5:16.

Therefore, I enjoin you to pray ceaselessly and fervently to keep self-righteousness out of your life. And if you already have the spirit of self-righteousness in your camp, know that it is a stranger and pray it out of your life, in the name of Jesus. **The word of God and prayer are potent spiritual weapons to overcome the spirit of self-righteousness** and to escape the judgment or punishments attached to it.

5. HAVE FAITH IN GOD

Finally, I would like you to always remember that "without faith, it is impossible to please God." Hebrew 11:6. You must believe God absolutely for your deliverance from self-righteousness. **You need faith**

to win life's battles. You need faith to destroy the works of the devil. You need faith to destroy visible and invisible barriers the enemy mounts in your way. You need faith to move from your Egypt to your Canaan. You need faith to conquer giants and part the Red Seas. **You need faith to fulfill your destiny and become all that God has destined you to be in Christ.** You need faith to dislodge the spirit of self-righteousness from your life church, home, organization, etc. The Bible says, "Call upon me and I will deliver you and you will glorify my name" (Psalm 50:15).

Mark 11:23-24

"For verily I say unto you, That whosoever shall say unto this mountain, Be thou removed, and be thou cast into the sea; and shall not doubt in his heart but shall believe that those things which he saith shall come to pass; he shall have whatsoever he saith. Therefore, I say unto you, What things soever ye desire, when ye pray, believe that ye receive them, and ye shall have them."

Beloved, keep on believing because God still answers prayers!

74

CONFESSION SECTION

DAILY DECLARATIONS OF RIGHTEOUSNESS

1. Father, I declare no weapon formed against me will prosper because I have the righteousness of Jesus Christ. – Isaiah 54:17

2. I declare that every tongue that rises up against me in judgment and condemnation. I have the right to condemn because I am righteous in Christ.

3. I declare that I have the Father's gift of righteousness; I will reign in life through Christ.

4. I declare that Abraham's blessings are mine, "Christ has redeemed us from the curse of the law, having become a curse for us (for it is written, cursed *is* everyone who hangs on a tree"), that the blessing of Abraham might come upon the Gentiles in Christ Jesus, that we might receive the promise of the Spirit through faith. – Galatians 3:13-14

5. I declare that I live by faith "For I am not ashamed of the gospel of Christ, for it is the power of God to salvation for everyone who believes, for the Jew first and also for the Greek. For in it the righteousness of God is revealed from faith to faith; as it is written, the just shall live by faith." - Romans 1:16-17

6. I declare that I am Filled with the fruit of righteousness that comes through Jesus Christ, to the glory and praise of God.

7. I declare that He who supplies seed to the Sower and bread for food will supply and multiply my seed for sowing and increase the harvest of His righteousness.

THANK YOU!

I'd like to use this time to thank you for purchasing my books and helping my ministry.

You have already accomplished so much, but I would appreciate an honest review of some of my books on your favorite retailer. This is critical since reviews reflect how much an author's work is respected.

Please be aware that I read and value all comments and reviews. You can always post a review even though you haven't finished the book yet and then edit your reviews later.

Thank you so much as you spare a precious moment of your time and may God bless you and meet you at the very point of your need.

Please send me an email at dr.pastormanny@gmail.com if you encounter any difficulty in leaving your review.

You can also send me an email at dr.pastormanny@gmail.com

If you need prayers or counsel or if you have questions. Better still if you want to be friends with me.

OTHER BOOKS BY EMMANUEL ATOE

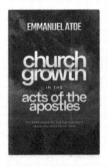

Church Growth in the Acts of the Apostles

The Church is the most powerful corporate body that is capable of commanding the attention of heaven on earth. The Church is God's idea and product, and so possesses an inbuilt capacity for success. The objective of this book is to get you acquainted with the purpose of the church in general, and the vision of Victory Sanctuary in particular.

A Moment of Prayer

There is nothing impossible with God but praying while breaking the law of God makes your prayers ineffective. Therefore, in this book, A Moment of Prayer, everyone under this program is expected to pray according to the rule, not against the law supporting it.

The Believer's Handbook

This book is highly recommendable for all. It is a book that will enhance your spiritual life, ignite the fire in you. It is a book that will open you heart to the mystery of faith.

The inestimable value of this book to every soul cannot be over emphasized. With this book you will get to know about the pillars of true faith in God. If you have been doubting your salvation, Christian life, the person and baptism of the Holy Ghost etc., this book is all you need.

Printed in the United States
by Baker & Taylor Publisher Services